ENDORSEMEN

Solid as a rock! That's what I thought as I read Marvin Yoder's book, *Revolutionary Mindset*. These pages are filled with practical wisdom that can be applied and produce remarkable results in our lives. What is especially beneficial is that what Marvin shares is not just wisdom, it's God's wisdom. Further, it is not just information that is correct, but it is full of life-transforming truth. You will enjoy Marvin's stories that illustrate how these very principles can help move your life up to a higher level.

TONY COOKE
Bible Teacher and author

This book, *Revolutionary Mindset*, challenges the reader to take control of their mind and emotions by regularly taking in the Word of God. To know and accomplish God's will in our lives has lot to do with what we read and listen to. This book teaches us how to build a positive mindset built on God's Word. I have known Marvin Yoder many years and have seen him live this in his life. He shares from his personal experiences how God has worked in his life. This is a great read!

SAM SMUCKER
Founder of The Worship Center
Lancaster, Pennsylvania

Whether a person is dealing with his health, provision, or even his emotions, *Revolutionary Mindset* is a step-by-step blueprint for going to the next level. I strongly recommend this book for anyone desiring to grow in the Christian life.

VAN CROUCH
Motivational Speaker and Author

I have known Marvin Yoder for a number of years. I have known him as a friend as well as a fellow minister of the Gospel of Christ. I have heard him speak, as well as reading his books and other ministry materials which are Bible-based. This book, *Revolutionary Mindset*, is no exception, and I highly recommend this book. I believe you will enjoy the truths you find and the practical wisdom that it contains.

CHARLES COWAN
Pastor of Faith Is The Victory Church
Nashville, Tennessee

In his book *Revolutionary Mindset*, Marvin Yoder reveals how you can intentionally transform your life according to the Word of God. So if you are ready to move to higher levels of living, then this book is definitely for you!

RONALD HARRISON, DDS

Marvin has done an excellent job in explaining many of the emotions and emotional makeup of humans. With this valuable knowledge, we can become a more complete man or woman of God.

LARRY PHALEN
Founder of Break Forth Bible Churches
Montana and North Dakota

In his book, Marvin Yoder does a great job of showing the power of the Word of God and the wonderful results and transformation that come from meditating on the Word. As you read this book, your mind will be renewed by the Word of God and your faith will grow. When you feed your faith on the Word of God, your life will change, mountains will be moved, and you will go to another supernatural level!

PASTOR MARK HANKINS

RENEW THE MIND

REVOLUTIONARY

STEP INTO A NEW SEASON

MINDSET

EXPERIENCE SUCCESS

MARVIN YODER

Published by Harrison House Publishers
Shippensburg, PA 17257

ISBN 13 TP: 978-1-6675-0327-1
ISBN 13 eBook: 978-1-6675-0328-8

For Worldwide Distribution, Printed in the USA.
1 2 3 4 5 6 7 8 / 28 27 26 25 24

DEDICATION

To my wife, Leah

To my daughters Christina, Nichole, and Audrey

To my Grandma Jemima

To my mom and dad

To all who believed in me through the years

Without all of you, I could not be who I am today

CONTENTS

FOREWORD

It is a great honor to recommend *Revolutionary Mindset,* written by Marvin Yoder. Our relationship began 41 years ago when Marvin became a Rhema Bible Training College student in 1982 and graduated in 1984.

Many years later, Marvin became an instructor at Rhema Bible Training College and on the pastoral staff at Rhema Bible Church. Through the years, I've watched his ministry grow and positively impact the Body of Christ. This book will be a blessing, and I highly recommend it.

Pastor Kenneth W. Hagin
Senior Pastor of Rhema Bible Church

PREFACE

"When we dream of things greater than our circumstances, it doesn't have to be in vain. That's how all great things begin. Now all that's left is to build it."

first realized this truth in elementary school, and that's when I realized it was possible to achieve things far beyond my present circumstances. So I dreamed about who I wanted to be and what I wanted to do in life. Then I set certain goals I wanted to accomplish for myself. Some were nothing more than childish dreams that never came to pass. Others were worthy of the effort it would take to reach them.

I soon discovered that dreams and goals don't happen automatically, nor are they easily accomplished. In the beginning I was quick to fault others or blame my upbringing or my circumstances. I used these things as excuses for why I didn't reach my goals. I even blamed God for allowing others to move ahead in life while I struggled along. However, when I became truthful to myself, I acknowledged that I was in control of my life and I needed God's help to reach my dreams and goals.

When you start on the journey toward becoming the person God planned for you to be, your life will begin to change dramatically. You'll come face to face with things in your life that you'll need to deal with. You may suddenly realize that your God-given potential and destiny is possible, and that it can come to pass. You may finally be able to move toward a dream or goal you've had for a long time.

The goal of this book is to present principles from the Bible concerning the soul—the mind, the will, and the emotions—and how to develop and enlarge the capacity of the soul to embrace all that God has promised in His Word.

The principles presented in this book are intended to help the normal development and growth in those who renew their mind, conform their will, and control their emotions. No psychiatric or clinical evaluation is implied or intended by these resources. This is not a definitive resource to help people with diagnosed disorders, emotional conditions that require medical supervision, or mental challenges that require professional help. We encourage people dealing with these type of things to seek professional help from a medical or psychiatric doctor or a professional counselor or psychologist.

As you look at the principles contained in this book, be honest with yourself. If you'll be truthful with yourself about who you are and the problems you have, God will be right there to help you. Sometimes it hurts to find out you're not as far along in life as you had thought. But when you're honest with God and yourself and admit you need His help, He will make it possible for you to experience the growth you desire.

INTRODUCTION

*"Obstacles can be conquered for
they are as big as they will ever
get, and we can overcome them
because we can keep on growing."*

'll never forget the first day I ventured out on one of the Rocky
Mountains. I had been in the Appalachian Mountains, the Smoky
Mountains, and even climbed a small mountain in Eastern Europe.
But the Rocky Mountain Range was much bigger and taller than any
other mountains I had seen! When I stood atop one of the Rocky
Mountains for the first time, I was frightened and overwhelmed.
Standing there looking down, it appeared that if I ever fell off the
mountain, I wouldn't stop falling for a long time. I felt out of control,
unable to function, and unfamiliar with the environment at that level.

After that first day up on the mountain, I went back to my
motel room not wanting to see another mountain for the rest of my

life! However, the next day I decided to spend the whole day in the mountains, because I didn't want fear, intimidation, or any other negative experiences to govern how I'd function in the future. After being at a higher altitude for the whole day, I became a little more familiar with the environment and how to do things there. I actually began to enjoy it. There is nothing like being elevated where you can see so much more and have a bigger perspective of the world around you!

I began to understand why many people don't want to move up in life. It's a different world when you are at a higher level. Overcoming fear of new heights, adjustments to an unfamiliar environment, and learning different principles and ways to do things are all a part of entering new realms. It is obvious that when you are at a higher altitude, whether on a mountain or in real life, what worked on a lower level will not work there.

Going to a higher level in life requires change. Most people go through life unconsciously responding to situations and challenges the way they have seen others do, by what others have told them, or based upon certain experiences they had in their growing up years. As life goes on, it becomes easy to acclimate to the circumstances without trying to rise above the existing limitations and boundaries. At some point, our life represents the attitudes we've cultivated rather than the circumstances or environment we find ourselves in. So changes within a person are necessary in order to successfully confront the challenges or situations around them.

Sir Edmund Hillary was a mountain climber from New Zealand who joined a British expedition to climb Mount Everest in 1951. They failed in their attempt that time, but later on in 1953 he and his Sherpa guide Tenzing Norgay were the first people known to successfully reach the 29,035-foot peak of Mount Everest.[1] For Sir Hillary to accomplish what no other man had done, he not only had to reach the peak of a mountain, but also to reach new peaks within himself. Changing what we want in life or rising up to walk in God's plan for our lives requires having a willingness to make adjustments in our thinking, to confront existing attitudes, and to establish new behavior patterns that allow us to move forward.

This book will help you get a perspective of how to move up to a new level of living. The truths presented here are based upon the principles in the Word of God, showing that it is God's idea for you to move up in life.

In this book, you'll find the main key to moving up higher in life. Following that, we'll break down each basic part of the human soul, see their basic functions, and how to change them to function better.

Finally, you'll discover some ideas and principles to help you develop into a better person, going from defensively fixing the broken down things that didn't work to offensively developing yourself so you can operate at a whole new level in life.

Is this book really for you? If you answer "yes" to the following questions, this book can help change your life!

- ▸ Are you ready to move beyond your current circumstances into a new realm of living that you've never experienced before?

- ▸ Are you ready to transform into the person God designed you to be?

- ▶ Do you want to learn how to control your thought life and tear down mental strongholds?

- ▶ Do you want to get off of the emotional roller coaster you have been riding?

- ▶ Do you want to position yourself for God to use you in a greater capacity?

- ▶ Do you want to get yourself ready to experience the promises of God in your life?

- ▶ Do you want to experience God's dream for your life instead of merely existing from one set of circumstances to another?

Then turn to Chapter 1: "Why Is My Life the Way It Is?"

NOTE

1. Encyclopedia Britannica, s.v. "Edmund Hillary," March 31, 2023, https://www.britannica.com/biography/Edmund-Hillary.

PART ONE

DISCOVERING THE KEY TO A NEW LIFE

Anyone who belongs to Christ has become a new person. The old life is gone; a new life has begun!

—THE APOSTLE PAUL, 2 CORINTHIANS 5:17 NLT

CHAPTER 1

WHY IS MY LIFE THE WAY IT IS?

"The purpose of life is not to see how long we can live, but in the difference we can make."

I was born and raised on a farm beside a county highway in an Amish family that believed in living separate from the world and focused on living within the Amish culture. However, every day I saw cars and trucks go by, and some of them I really liked a lot. I also read almost every library book in the little school I attended. Every year I looked intently through the big Sears and Roebuck catalog that came in the mail, looking at all the things I wanted to have. I had a curious mind that led me to explore things, ask questions, and try new things. There was a big world out there, and I wanted to be a part of it.

Many people go through life focused only on achieving their dreams and getting their share of riches and wealth in this world.

However, the most important thing is to focus on becoming the person we were created to be and walking in God's plan for our lives. God's desire for us is to move up to what He promised us in His Word and to know that today is not a life sentence. Within the framework of His will, God wants to help us break into the next level of living, provision, and health.

MY SEARCH FOR A BETTER LIFE

A number of years ago, I found myself endeavoring to do what I believed was God's will for me and my family. Although I was walking with God the best I knew how, I was struggling, trying to make ends meet, and my family was doing without a lot of things they should have had. We lived in a house so ugly we never took any pictures of it.

I kept wondering what I was doing wrong, because we weren't experiencing God's blessings as I believed we could. God's promises in the Bible painted a radically different picture than the situation we were living in. I tried to exercise faith to receive God's blessings, but it seemed that something was sabotaging my efforts—something worked against me that kept us from receiving what we needed.

Sometimes I wondered if things would ever get any better. Thoughts came to my mind that I probably couldn't handle a better life than what we currently had. Years passed by, and we continued to live at about the same level in life and nothing seemed to change much. I finally got so tired of the way things were that I began to seek God and His Word with even greater fervor. I thought to myself that if there were any answers that would help me, they were in God's Word! I searched for almost two years before I came across a verse in the Bible that shed some light on my situation and gave me a hope for the future.

GOD SPEAKS THROUGH HIS WORD

The apostle John may not have fully realized the significance of the greeting he penned in his letter to Gaius that we know as 3 John 1:2 (NKJV), *"Beloved, I pray that you may prosper in all things and be in health, just as your soul prospers."* His greeting expressed God's will for all His children so accurately that God included it in the canon of His Holy Word for His children. The Epistle of 3 John may have originally been a letter from one man to another, but when God included it in His Word it became a divine word that speaks to us today.

Probably everyone agrees that Jesus' words in John 3:16 are for us today even though He was speaking to Nicodemus when He said it. In the same way, even though in 3 John 1:2 John greeted a man named Gaius, this verse also applies to us today. Every verse in the Bible is *"given by inspiration of God, and is profitable for doctrine, for reproof, for correction, for instruction in righteousness"* (2 Timothy 3:16 NKJV).

In 3 John 1:2, we see God expressing His will for our lives, which includes prosperity and health. Just as John 3:16 declares God's will for all sinners to be saved, 3 John 1:2 declares God's will for all Christians to be well provided for and healthy in their Christian journey. God has expressed His will for us in this verse, and now it's up to us to receive His will into our lives.

GOD REVEALS HIS WILL TO US

Many people think only of money when someone brings up the subject of *prosperity*. However, we all know of people who have lots of money and wealth, but they don't serve God. So when God mentions prosperity in a positive way in His Word, no doubt He is referring to a lot more than just money or material wealth. Actually, the concept of biblical prosperity includes our spiritual progress, the well-being of our family, and doing well in our ministries and employment as much as it involves being successful in our finances. It also includes being obedient to do God's will and obeying His Word. Prosperity really includes almost everything we're involved in. So there is much more to prosperity than just having money.

The Greek word used in 3 John 1:2 for "prosper" is the word *eudoo*, and it gives the idea of experiencing continuing prosperity over a period of time. It also points toward a person succeeding in reaching the destination of their journey and being successful in their endeavors. From this we can see that God's idea of prosperity is not just about money. His definition of prosperity includes for us to do well on our Christian journey, just as John wanted Gaius to do well on his journey through life.

The word *health* includes our physical well-being, our mental and emotional state, as well as our strength and energy. Our health is important because it allows us to do whatever God tells us to do. Just as Gaius needed to be healthy to reach the destination of his journey, so we need to be healthy to complete our Christian journey.

DETERMINE WHAT IS IMPORTANT

Someone may ask, "Isn't salvation more important than prosperity and health?" If a person is not born again, then certainly salvation is more important. However, since this verse is written to Christians, it reveals that two very important issues for us are prosperity and health in fulfilling the will of God.

Why is our prosperity and health so important to God? God knows that when we are prosperous and healthy we are in the best possible position to obey Him. Some people may have a desire to obey

God, but they can't because they lack the resources to do so. People who are not healthy may want to serve God, but they are physically limited. God is not against a person because he is poor or sick. He has provided the answer for poverty and sickness, and He wants to help people move out of these things. God has done that because those who have good health are more able to obey God and do His will.

Some people have the mistaken idea that their sickness or poverty enables them to be better witnesses for Christ in the earth. Perhaps in the midst of these conditions, these people do have opportunities to share their faith with others. But how much more could they do if they were free from sickness and poverty and had the physical ability and the resources to obey whatever God told them to do? When we have the prosperity and health God has promised in His Word, we are able to accomplish much more for the kingdom of God.

GOD'S WILL IS NOT AUTOMATIC

While God's will for us is prosperity and health, these things don't happen automatically in our lives. There are conditions to be met. Concerning 3 John 1:2, Matthew Poole wrote, "He reckons he might well make the prosperous state of his soul the measure of all the other prosperity he could wish unto him."[1] Within this verse, although historically it is a greeting from the apostle John to a man named Gaius, there is a guiding principle stated that governs how people live in prosperity and health. God desires for us to focus on having a prosperous soul, which in turn allows us to successfully experience material things and good health. So it appears that the safeguard that God has placed within humankind pertaining to their ability to walk in prosperity and health is the condition of their soul.

Some people attempt to prosper financially by winning the lottery. However, lotteries award large sums of money to individuals on the basis of a winning ticket instead of having a prosperous soul. Consequently, many who have won large sums of money in a lottery now have ruined lives because they received great increase, which exceeded the condition of their soul. This led them to make poor decisions about what to do with their money and spend it on things that were detrimental to their well-being. Or they did not make wise investments and lost their money as a result. This is a picture of what happens when the equation in 3 John 1:2 is out of balance.

Someone may say, "If God blesses us too much, I'm afraid we'll forget God." Proverbs 10:22 (NKJV) tells us that *"The blessing of the Lord makes one rich, and He adds no sorrow with it."* In other words, God will not bless you beyond the level of what your soul can handle. Problems occur only when people pursue prosperity and neglect their relationship with God. When we know the condition of our soul is the standard for us experiencing prosperity in all other areas of our lives, we can be assured that God's blessings will be for our good and not for our destruction.

DISCOVER A LIFE-CHANGING EQUATION

Look at 3 John 1:2 (NKJV) again: *"Beloved, I pray that you may prosper in all things and be in health, just as your soul prospers."* In this verse, John indicates a relationship between the condition of a person's soul and their prosperity and health. He said our prosperity and health are *"just as"* our soul prospers—not "more than" or "less than." A mathematician might state the relationship shown in this verse in the form of an equation, which would look like this:

OUR PROSPERITY AND HEALTH = THE CONDITION OF OUR SOUL

An equation always has two equal sides. If one part is changed and not the other, the equation is no longer true. Most of the promises in God's Word have a "God side" and a "human side," and both sides must be completed in order for that promise to manifest in our life. Therefore, if we change the "condition of the soul" side in this equation, God will change the "prosperity and health" side. Several truths can be learned from this equation.

First of all, the health and prosperity we actually experience in this life are governed by the condition of our soul. It is impossible for us to continually walk in a level of health and prosperity that exceeds the condition of our soul.

Second, in our heart we may know the will of God for our life, but the condition of our soul will determine what we will actually experience in life. It is true that God said in His Word that all His promises are for us, but the condition of our soul will actually determine if we experience those promises.

Third, we can know a truth in our heart, but if we're not convinced of it in our soul, we will not operate in it because the soul is where the decisions of life are made.

Knowing this equation takes the mystery out of operating in the prosperity, health, and increase that God promised to us in His Word. We can start on the road to God's will for our life whenever we choose by changing the condition of our soul. We begin by changing our thinking. The power to change our soul is within our reach by reading the Word of God and receiving the help of the

Holy Spirit. We can decide that today is the first day of changing the condition of our soul and experiencing new levels of living.

IDENTIFYING THE REAL PROBLEM

Our real problem is not our boss, our parents, our environment, or our upbringing. Our greatest problem is located between our two ears—in our soul. The good news is that since our primary problem is the condition of our soul, we can do something about it. Our problem is not beyond our reach. We don't have to stay the same; we can start changing the condition of our soul whenever we want.

We're not talking about things beyond a person's control. For example, a person has no control over their upbringing, the environment in which they grew up, or the decisions made by their parents. Accidents happen and trouble comes knocking on everyone's door.

However, possessing a prosperous soul will enable us to respond in a scriptural manner, when things do happen to us, and allow God to have the last word in our situation. We may not have been in control of our past, but we can take charge of our future by developing a prosperous soul so that the will of God can come to pass in our life.

What we actually experience in life concerning the will of God can be determined and measured by the condition of your soul. The well-being of our soul then is the key to our spiritual, mental, physical, financial, and social progress in life because that is where the decisions of life are made. It affects every area of our lives.

We must keep several things in mind as we pursue God and attempt to move up into the increase and realms of living He has promised us in His Word. There is the aspect of simply knowing who God is and what He has for us. Another aspect is the law of sowing and reaping. Yet another aspect to obtaining God's increase is having faith in His Word. Also, the anointing and the miraculous power of the Holy Spirit play a part in receiving increase. However, unless we develop a prosperous soul, all these other aspects of obtaining increase from God will be difficult, if not impossible, to walk in and maintain in our lives. Right thinking is a prerequisite and a priority if we are going to successfully function in these other areas of increase and move up to new realms of living.

Notice what John wrote in 3 John 1:3 (NKJV), *"For I rejoiced greatly when brethren came and testified of the truth that is in you, just as you walk in the truth."* In verse 2, John states the necessity of a prosperous soul. In verse 3, John said he rejoiced greatly when he heard that his fellow Christians have the truth, or the Word of God, in them. This reveals that having a prosperous soul and having the truth in you are synonymous. Apart from having the Word of God in you, it is impossible to have a truly prosperous soul.

Depositing the Word of God in our soul on a daily basis is necessary to develop a prosperous soul. Anything else would be less than what God wants for us. We know we have the truth in us when it shows up in our lifestyle, influences who we associate with and the places we go, and changes our countenance and our attitudes. When the Word of God becomes a part of our soul, it creates a ripple effect that brings real change in all the other areas of our life.

OUR HEALTH AND WELL-BEING

The condition of our soul affects our health and well-being. Often the condition of the physical body can give some insight as to how good or bad our soul is functioning. Some of the medical field is acknowledging that there is a connection between our physical health and the condition of our souls. Internalizing or holding within us thoughts about the wrong things others have done to us or about the unfair things that happened to us in life can lead to developing a wrong set of attitudes. Eventually all of this will create problems in our physical bodies. Attitudes such as bitterness, unforgiveness, hatred, or jealousy over a period of time can create negative effects upon the physical body.

Proverbs 17:22 (NKJV) says, *"A merry heart does good, like medicine, but a broken spirit dries the bones."* Also Proverbs 4:20-23 (NKJV) tells us:

> *My son, give attention to my words; incline your ear to my sayings. Do not let them depart from your eyes; keep them in the midst of your heart; for they are life to those who find them, and health to all their flesh. Keep your heart with all diligence, for out of it spring the issues of life.*

These verses reveal that the condition of your soul has an effect upon your physical body.

OUR ACHIEVEMENTS AND DESTINY

The condition of our soul also has an effect upon our achievements and our ultimate destiny in life. We tend to move in the direction of what we predominantly think about. If we change our thought life, it becomes the beginning of changing the world we live in. By this, we mean that our constant thoughts and meditations will create the atmosphere around us in which we live. Thoughts alone may not change our world, but they are seeds that are capable of producing fruit. When we water our constant thoughts with our imagination and add faith and hard work, we will often see the reality of those thoughts in our lives. Genesis 1:11-12 reveals the principle of seed-time and harvest, which we can also apply to our thought life.

What we allow into our soul and store there will determine what kind of person we eventually become. We are a product of the thoughts we think continually, the imaginations we entertain, and what we choose to remember of the past. We must choose carefully what we bring into our mind, for it will greatly determine what we believe is possible for us to achieve in life.

On May 6, 1954, at Iffley Road stadium at Oxford, Roger Bannister was the first person to officially run a mile in 3 minutes and 59.04 seconds. By doing this, he broke the seemingly impossible four-minute mile barrier. Indeed, Bannister had been told by physiologists that not only was running the four-minute mile impossible for an athlete to do, but attempting to do so was dangerous to one's health. As is so often the case with world records, once Bannister proved a human could in fact run a mile under four minutes, it left the world stunned and helped shatter a collective mental barrier. Within a month, Australian John Landy bettered the Iffley Road record with a time of 3 minutes 57.9 seconds. In the next several years that followed that historic day in Oxford, numerous other runners also performed the same feat.[2]

OUR FINANCIAL PROSPERITY

The measure of financial and business success we are able to achieve in this life is greatly determined by the condition of our soul. Our success and promotion may depend more upon our attitude toward the company than in our ability to do the work. Even if we don't qualify for the "technical expertise" path to promotion, we can still qualify by being in the "good attitude" line. We need to think and believe thoughts like *If God is for us, who can be against us?* (Romans 8:31 NKJV). This will help us maintain a good attitude and rise above the attacks of doubt, condemnation, or fear that try to talk us out of the possibility of making any progress or receiving a promotion.

Some people resist change. Someone said these people are "like concrete: thoroughly mixed up and absolutely set!" However, our soul must change if we want our prosperity and health to improve. We must begin to embrace new thoughts from God's Word to change our thinking of what is possible for us to do. As we enlarge our mind with thoughts from God's Word, we can embrace what God tells us to do.

AS WE THINK IN OUR SOUL

Many people are not willing to spend money to change their thinking, and therefore their level of believing what they can do doesn't change. Some people are willing to spend tens of thousands of dollars on a vehicle that will decrease in value and eventually wear out, but they won't spend a hundred dollars to go to a seminar that would improve their mind and enlarge their thought process. Improving the condition of our soul can happen when we're willing to spend money to go to school and buy books, audio, and video products and begin to feed on them. The information we received from them will change our soul.

We must let our mind be stretched to embrace new ideas and think larger thoughts than we ever dared to think before. Changing our thinking helps us to embrace dreams so big that they're beyond our human ability, and the only way they can become a reality is if God does it by the power of His Spirit.

Our whole life is governed by how our soul functions. When we enlarge our mind with new thoughts and ideas, we are forever changed. The truth is, our destinies are decided many years before the actual events occur because of the thoughts, ideas, imaginations, and memories that we allow to dwell continually in our soul. King Solomon said, *"For as he thinks in his soul, so is he"* (Proverbs 23:7 ABPS).

NOTES

1. Matthew Poole, *Annotations upon the Holy Bible: wherein the sacred text is inserted, and various readings annexed, together with the parallel Scriptures*, Vol. 3, (New York: R. Carter and Brothers, 1852), 942.

2. *Encyclopedia Britannica*, s.v. "Roger Bannister," March 19, 2023, https://www.britannica.com/biography/Roger-Bannister.

CHAPTER 2

THE KEY TO A NEW LIFE

*"God created the human soul
to be a great repository out of
which we can mine great riches."*

In my family, higher education was not encouraged because of our religious beliefs. Yet I was always curious about things, asking questions, and challenging the boundaries of our culture. Even though I had no formal education beyond middle school until later in life, I was always trying to learn something new. I imagined driving a car, pondered how an airplane works, and tried to build a guitar. I dreamed of playing major league baseball, being a cowboy, or becoming an FBI agent. Often what was going on in my mind was a lot different from the life I was actually living. People around me saw me only as a young kid trying to find his way in life, often mischievous and causing problems. But I saw myself doing great things.

Often we only think of the visible part a person—the physical body that we can see. People usually make up their mind about a person based on what they see—their physical stature, the way they dress, the manner in which they conduct themselves, etc. But there is far more to the makeup of a person than just the physical body. Man is actually made up of three basic parts: spirit, soul, and body. In the New Testament, the word *soul* usually refers to the inward part of a person. It is the place where we find a person's thoughts, imaginations, attitudes, affections, desires, and passions. From the soul come expressions of love or hatred, patience or anger, kindness or jealousy, compassion or bitterness, and forgiveness or unforgiveness. Thus a person will eventually become a representative of what is in their soul.

THE WORD BRINGS UNDERSTANDING

Lack of biblical understanding and failing to identify the distinct qualities of the soul and the spirit of a person has led some Christian scholars to conclude that the soul and spirit are the same. Thus they came to view humankind as a dichotomy—a two-part being. However, a careful study of the Word of God shows they are not the same. Notice in the following Scriptures the soul and spirit are mentioned separately as two distinct parts of a human being.

> *Now may the God of peace Himself sanctify you completely; and may your whole spirit, soul, and body be preserved blameless at the coming of our Lord Jesus Christ* (1 Thessalonians 5:23 NKJV).

> *For the word of God is living and powerful, and sharper than any two-edged sword, piercing even to the division of soul and spirit, and of joints and marrow, and is a*

discerner of the thoughts and intents of the heart (Hebrews 4:12 NKJV).

These Scriptures present man as a person with three major parts. Humankind doesn't just consist of the physical part that we can see. There are three major divisions or three definite components of a human being—spirit, soul, and body. These verses give us insight concerning knowing who we are, which is necessary for successfully preparing and dealing with issues and situations in life.

IDENTIFY THE PARTS OF THE SOUL

The word *soul* is used several ways in the Word of God. Sometimes it refers to the whole being of a person, such as in Acts 2:43 (NKJV): *"Then fear came upon every soul, and many wonders and signs were done through the apostles."* It may also refer to certain people or a group of people, i.e., 1 Peter 3:20 (NKJV): *"in the days of Noah, while the ark was being prepared, in which a few, that is, eight souls, were saved through water."* In many places in Scripture, the soul refers to a part of the makeup of humanity, as Psalm 23:3 (NKJV) tells us, *"He restores my soul; He leads me in the paths of righteousness for His name's sake."*

We can identify three major parts within the human soul: the mind, the will, and the emotions. Other less noticeable parts of the soul exist that are typically related or connected to one or more of these major parts. However, our studies will concentrate primarily on these three major parts. God wants our mind to be transformed by His Word, our will to be conformed to His will, and our emotions to be stabilized so we can freely follow His leading. These major parts of the soul will be defined in greater depth later on.

GET THE RIGHT KIND OF HELP

Having a basic understanding of the purpose and function of the soul and its various parts enables us to incorporate real change in our lives and begin to experience the best that God has for us. Because of simple lack of knowledge, or misunderstanding, many people are living lives that are unfulfilled and packed with frustration. They are living far below the level of God's will and promises.

We can only maximize our relationship with God and move up to the level of living where God planned for us to be when we understand what goes on in our soul and begin to operate in the principles of God's Word to bring change within us.

God can bless a person when they get the right kind of help. Psalm 1:1 reads, *"Blessed is the man who walks not in the counsel of the ungodly."* This means when we need counseling, we should find someone who can give sound advice according to the godly principles of the Word of God and the leading of the Holy Spirit. This helps us to make our way prosperous and be successful.

THE HOLY SPIRIT WILL HELP US

The Holy Spirit is called *Counselor* in John 14:16 (AMPC), and He will counsel you according to the Word of God, often through another godly person. We're not talking about just using our willpower and strength to change ourselves. We must incorporate the Word of God as the foundation for any positive, lasting change in our soul.

As Christians, we are not to rely upon just the natural things of this world for help with our soul. This kind of help at best is only temporary. Several years ago the word *psychobabble* came into existence, referring to psychological jargon, often trivial or worthless, that brings no lasting value or change. Some people freely share their advice, whether it is of any value or not. While secular counsel has some value, often it is limited in how much it can lead a person to experience lasting, permanent change. Often they can tell us what the problem or symptoms are and how to manage or control them, but they can't provide the inner change that only comes from God's Word and His Spirit.

A number of years ago a friend of mine was having some problems, so he went to a psychologist for help. After spending hundreds of dollars for numerous sessions with the psychologist, the psychologist told my friend what his problems were. Later my friend told me, "I needed more than that. What I needed were real answers to those problems!"

PEACE IN OUR SOUL

The well-being of our soul is directly related to having the peace of God in our mind and heart. Having the peace of God begins with receiving Christ as our Lord and Savior, for He is our peace (see Ephesians 2:14). However, the condition of our soul, which is often determined by our circumstances, environment, relatives, childhood upbringing, level of social status, or degree of education, will greatly determine how much of God's peace we will actually experience in life.

If we allow these issues in our past to affect our soul until we predominantly live our lives in the light of them, we will lack God's peace and live far below the level on which God wants us to be. The great battles of life often take place in the soul of a person, where satan often attacks us in our soulish arena via our thoughts, imaginations, and attitudes.

What we allow to reside in our soul, either from the Word of God or from satan, often decides the outcome of our life. Satan tries to rob us of our peace of mind so that we don't flow with the will of God for our life. However, God has given us His Word so we can walk according to His will and experience peace of mind. If we can win the battle in our mind, the battles in other areas will be much easier to win.

BE SELECTIVE OF OUR THOUGHTS

The apostle Paul wrote:

> And the peace of God, which surpasses all understanding, will guard your hearts and minds through Christ Jesus. Finally, brethren, whatever things are true, whatever things are noble, whatever things are just, whatever things are pure, whatever things are lovely, whatever things are of good report, if there is any virtue and if there is anything praiseworthy—meditate on these things (Philippians 4:7-8 NKJV).

Being selective of the thoughts that we dwell upon is part of the process of improving the condition of our soul. This makes it possible for us to experience more of God's peace in our lives. The more we focus our thoughts on the Word of God, the greater God's peace will manifest in our life. Psalm 119:165 (NKJV) reveals that, *"Great peace have those who love Your law, and nothing causes them to stumble."*

PRESERVING OUR SOUL

A person who has no peace of mind is someone who has not received Christ as their Savior, or they may have put wrong information in their mind that is contrary to the Word of God. This leads to negative thoughts of fear, doubt, condemnation, guilt, shame, etc. Often they haven't consistently, on a regular basis, put the Word of God in their mind and heart until it gives them assurance that God will take care of them and everything will be all right. We must realize the level of peace in our mind greatly depends upon the level to which we have implanted the principles and promises of God's Word into our minds.

First Thessalonians 5:23 (NKJV) states that, *"Now may the God of peace Himself sanctify you completely; and may your whole spirit, soul, and body be preserved blameless at the coming of our Lord Jesus Christ."* This verse reveals the value of the peace of God, which is able to preserve our whole being—spirit, soul, and body. In other words, our soul will experience no rest from the attacks of the enemy and the pressures of life until it experiences the peace that comes from God.

The peace of God is able to preserve our soul even in the midst of trying times. In the midst of great personal tragedy, when he lost his whole family, Horatio G. Spafford penned the words to the great hymn that is still sung today:

> When peace like a river attendeth my way,
> When sorrows like sea billows roll,
> Whatever my lot, thou hast taught me to say,
> It is well, it is well with my soul.[1]

Our daily focus should be on the well-being of our soul. This requires both making sure our soul gets relief from the strain and stress of life as well as verbally affirming the peace of God over our mind, will, and emotions. The peace of God is truly vital to the well-being of our souls.

MAINTAINING PEACE OF MIND

The way we maintain peace of mind is to choose our thoughts that we continually and repeatedly dwell on. What we choose to continually think about ultimately determines the condition of our soul. That's why the Bible tells us what to think on.

> *Finally, brethren, whatever things are true, whatever things are noble, whatever things are just, whatever things are pure, whatever things are lovely, whatever things are of good report, if there is any virtue and if there is anything praiseworthy—meditate on these things* (Philippians 4:8 NKJV).

There are things that are true, but they are not lovely, nor do they have a good report. There are things that are honest, but there is neither praise nor virtue (admirable quality, merit, or moral excellence) exhibited in them. For example, it may be a true and honest report that the crime rate in America is higher than it was 30 years ago, but this is not a good report, nor a lovely situation. It has no praise or virtue in it. Therefore, dwelling continually upon that report can cause us to become fearful and lose our peace of mind.

CHOOSE WHAT GOES INTO THE SOUL

We can purposefully focus our thoughts and imaginations in the direction of God's Word until His will for us becomes a stronghold in our soul. The apostle Paul shows us a picture of how thoughts can grow and have a strong hold of our lives when he wrote:

> *For the weapons of our warfare are not carnal but mighty in God for pulling down strongholds, casting down arguments and every high thing that exalts itself against the*

*knowledge of God, bringing every thought into captivity
to the obedience of Christ* (2 Corinthians 10:4-5 NKJV).

A process occurs in our soul in which thoughts that we continually dwell upon lead to imaginations. As we continue to entertain these imaginations, eventually they become strongholds in our soul. This process works to produce either positive or negative results, depending upon the thoughts we dwell on.

Imaginations are our human ability to create thoughts, ideas, concepts, and pictures apart from the physical world around us. From our imaginations we get images, concepts, and vision to help us move beyond our present problems and circumstances. People from all walks of life—rich or poor, young and old, free and not free—are able to use their imagination to envision a new life.

Depending upon what images we allow in our mind during the process of imagination, we will either be lifted up into the peace God has given to us, or we will find ourselves experiencing a lifestyle far below what He intended for us. If we dwell upon these images long enough, they'll become etched in our soul until they become strongholds in our mind and in our life.

BUILDING CASTLES IN THE SOUL

What is a stronghold in the human soul? The Greek meaning of the word *stronghold* stronghold in 2 Corinthians 10:4-5 gives the idea of something very strong, like a castle. In the natural a castle is a very strong, safe, defensive place where people go to for safety from the enemy. In medieval times, castles were built with strong and very sturdy building material, appearing to be impregnable and almost impossible to conquer.

Strong attitudes and habitual thought patterns eventually become the castles we build in our soul. This is why our attitudes and thought patterns seem so impregnable and fortified until they look like they're unchangeable. These things have obtained a stronghold or grip in our soul, and seemingly our thinking, will, and emotions are unalterable. Thus many people conclude that the way they are can't be improved.

Attitudes don't appear overnight any more than a castle is built in a day. Attitudes emerge from imaginations entertained, and imaginations are thoughts dwelled upon. Thought is the seed of attitudes, and imaginations are the soil in which attitudes grow.

Over time we build our own thoughts and habits, and then our thoughts and habits eventually make us who we are. In a real sense, we are our own builders. We have to deal with both removing old thoughts and habits and building new thoughts and attitudes within us. How do we tear down a negative, harmful attitude that has become a fortress or castle in our soul? The answer is found in the way it is built.

A castle is built one stone at a time. Stones become walls, and walls become castles. In the same way, our attitudes are built one thought at a time. If we want to tear down old thoughts and build new ones in our soul, we must do it one thought at a time. Remember, the process starts with a thought, becomes an imagination, and eventually forms a stronghold in our soul.

For example, no one decides on the spur of the moment that they are going to commit an act of adultery. Such an act is the product of thoughts unchecked in a person's mind until they imagine the event in their mind. After a while, these thoughts become a stronghold in their mind and lead that person to commit the actual physical event. Every action is preceded by a thought; thus, the thought is the seed that is capable of bringing forth the action.

We can change any attitude or thought pattern by understanding this process. The thoughts of God's Word conform the attitudes and thought patterns in our soul into a fortress of peace. Changing the thoughts, imaginations, and attitudes in our soul will gradually cause us to experience a new life we never had before!

Our soul can be changed, either for good or bad, through a process over a period of time. Every thought, imagination, idea, or memory is important because it can either add to or take away from our peace of mind, our relationship with God, and is a factor in us rising up to the life that God wants us to live.

NOTE

1. Horatio Gates Spafford, "It is Well With My Soul," 1873, www .loc.gov/item/mamcol.016.

PART TWO

DEFINING THE HUMAN SOUL WITHIN US

I will pursue your commands, for you expand my understanding.

—KING DAVID, PSALM 119:32 NLT

CHAPTER 3

HOW OUR MIND WORKS

"A human is distinct from all other creatures by having a soul with rational thoughts and expressions, which must be brought under the divine instruction of God to move in the right direction."

grew up without television, so after I left home and moved into my own place, I began to avidly watch television, even the reruns because they were all new to me. Almost every week I watched a comedy and music show called *Hee Haw*. On the show they sang a lot of somewhat pessimistic country and western songs with catchy melodies and had lots of corny humor filled with verbal jabs and put-downs. Consequently, after watching the show for a while, I began to sing parts of those songs and use the same kind of humor. After about six months, without realizing it, my expectations and conduct in life began to reflect the negative, pessimistic things that were said on that show, as well as some other shows I had watched. I went around expecting, "Doom and gloom and agony on me…if it weren't for bad luck I'd have no luck at all." In retrospect, what I had listened to and watched shaped the way my mind worked and influenced the way I thought about everything in life, what I believed, what I accomplished, and who I chose to be my friends.

Many people don't realize the things they're watching, listening, and paying attention to over a period of time will become a huge factor in what they will experience in life. To have a prosperous soul, we must know how our mind works and how to take care of it. Our mind has to function correctly if we are going to move to new levels of living. In this book, we're not going to look at how to fix major disorders or problems at a psychologist/psychiatrist level. We are simply going to look at what the Word of God has to say about the mind, how it functions, and how we can learn to make good decisions in life.

WE'RE NOT ALL THE SAME

The Bible mentions various kinds of minds, which helps us realize the different conditions that are possible for people's minds to be in. The Word of God speaks of people having carnal or fleshly minds (Romans 8:6-7; Colossians 2:18), reprobate minds (Romans 1:28), corrupt minds (1 Timothy 6:5; 2 Timothy 3:8), doubtful minds (Luke 12:29), despiteful minds (Ezekiel 36:5), and those who are double-minded (James 1:8; 4:8).

On the other hand, the Word of God instructs believers to be sober-minded (Titus 2:6), have a lowly or humble mind (Acts 17:11; 2 Corinthians 8:12; 1 Peter 5:2), and to be pure minded (2 Peter 3:1). God wants believers to have a sound mind (2 Timothy

1:7) and to have spiritual minds, or the mind of Christ (Romans 8:6,27; 12:2; 1 Corinthians 2:16).

Understanding that people have various kinds of mindsets and conditions helps us understand why trouble abounds in the world. These different kinds of minds are the products of the thoughts that people have entertained over a period of time. Therefore, their minds think differently, have different values and beliefs, and have different goals. Their likes and dislikes are different, and this often causes disagreements and arguments to take place.

DIFFERENT KINDS OF MINDS

Have you ever stopped to think how many different kinds of minds are present in just one room full of people? This is one reason why disagreements and difficulties take place in families and organizations, including churches. It contributes to one person having certain social, political, or religious perspectives and their siblings having different or opposing views. It's why different people express various opinions at the coffee shop. The condition of the mind explains why a person expresses themselves with greater or lesser passion about a subject or project. Whatever mindset we have developed over a period of time greatly determines our approach to life and explains why some people are super achievers while others barely accomplish anything.

God has some very clear instructions about the way we as Christians are to be. The Word of God instructs us to *"be perfectly joined together in the same mind and in the same judgment"* (1 Corinthians 1:10 NKJV). When people are of the same mind, it enables them to have mutual thinking and make decisions collectively. All of the people in a group or on a team may not agree on everything and may have to agree to disagree on some things. Yet with effort all involved can focus their minds on the commonly held ideas and beliefs. This makes it possible for people to have similar evaluations or judgments, reach the same conclusions, and take a harmonious course of action.

RECEIVING AND GIVING OUT INFORMATION

Our mind is where we store information. The mind is capable, either on a conscious or subconscious level, to remember all we have ever learned. It also assimilates the knowledge in our thoughts and imaginations to lead our human will to either submit or rebel, and it helps us govern or freely express our emotions and feelings.

Our mind is like a recorder that basically does two things. It records new information or plays back what has been recorded. We can choose which function is activated. Too often people simply play recorded information (remembering the past) instead of recording new material to replace the old (gathering new information via their thoughts and imaginations).

The way we are is due in part to the genetics that we inherited from our parents. However, the information brought into our mind and stored there also plays a vital part in determining what kind of person we eventually become. Proverbs 23:7 (NKJV) states that *"For as he thinks in his heart, so is he."* Many people have risen above the dictates of their genetic makeup by selecting certain thought processes and continually entertaining them in their mind until they became a reality in their life.

OUR THOUGHTS EVENTUALLY DEFINE US

We are a product of the thoughts we think continually, the imaginations we entertain, and the memories of the past that we choose to remember. Idle thoughts do not exist; every thought contributes toward forming our true self. Eventually, our habitual thoughts will express themselves in words and deeds. Our choices in life become a reflection of what we have been thinking in our minds.

We must choose carefully what we bring into our mind. One of our most powerful moments is when we choose what kind of information we allow into our mind. Our destiny is largely decided by a thought, an imagination, an idea, or a memory that we continually dwell upon.

Viktor E. Frankl was an Austrian psychotherapist who was imprisoned in Nazi concentration camps from 1942 to 1945 during the Holocaust in World War II. Later, he observed that although everything else had been taken away from him, he still had the ability to select certain attitudes in his mind. If anyone would be qualified to make this statement, it would be a person who survived such terrible atrocities and dire, life-threatening circumstances as he did. In fact, what he said shows that choosing our attitudes in the midst of trying times is a real key to surviving the ordeals we're going through.

HOW THE MIND GATHERS INFORMATION

The mind is affected or changed through a process and not instantaneously changed like our human spirit can be. God continually works to get the right information into our conscious thinking. What God does in our soul doesn't happen instantaneously, but through a process over a period of time. Through daily application of the Word, our mind will grow in increasing knowledge about God, His Word, and His grace to walk in His will.

The mind gathers information in two ways: 1) via the conscience, and 2) by the five physical senses. The mind receives information through the conscience in our heart where the Holy Spirit resides. The conscience brings knowledge from the spirit realm, guides us in the will of God, and shows us right and wrong according to God's Word.

THE WORLD APPEALS TO OUR PHYSICAL SENSES

The five physical senses also bring information from the physical body and the physical world we live in. For example, the sense of touch is designed to send a message to our mind warning us not to touch the burner on the stove when it is hot. The mind then makes a decision not to touch the hot burner and controls the members of the body to stay away from it. Through the sense of taste, the mind decides whether it likes or dislikes certain foods and if the body should eat more of that food or reject it. In the same way, when a person experiences pain, the sense of touch or nerves in the body send a message to the mind to get help, to get away, or to go where it is safe.

The world appeals to our sense of sight and hearing to send information to our mind. It tries to influence our thinking, either to gain our support or to desensitize us toward a particular issue or product. Businesses utilize the sense of sight to sell their products, displaying them online, in newspapers, television, and on billboards.

OUR MIND IS CONSTANTLY WORKING

It seems that the sense of sight sends the strongest messages from the physical realm to the mind. People are often moved by what they see. For example, if you put green food coloring on a perfectly cooked steak, almost no one will want to eat it, even though there's nothing harmful about it. This is why television and Internet have become such effective mediums to convey information in our society. Movies are also a powerful factor in shaping people's thoughts and conditioning their minds to certain beliefs and behaviors.

The mind gathers information continuously and updates its information files, often by what the sense of sight and hearing tell it. The things people see and hear move them to think certain thoughts, go into a particular direction, or do specific things. Even the devil uses the sense of sight to get people to see certain things so they'll respond the way he wants them to.

This helps us see the value of daily devotions in God's Word. This is why the apostle Paul wrote, *"And do not be conformed to this world, but be transformed by the renewing of your mind, that you may prove what is that good and acceptable and perfect will of God"* (Romans 12:2 NKJV). As we renew our mind, we delete old information files and create new information files in our mind according to the Word.

SOUL AND SPIRIT WORK DIFFERENTLY

Spiritual things—such as receiving salvation, forgiveness, or a miracle—can happen instantly. When a person becomes born again, their human spirit is instantly recreated: *"Therefore, if anyone is in Christ, he is a new creation; old things have passed away; behold, all things have become new"* (2 Corinthians 5:17 NKJV). The moment we receive salvation though Jesus Christ and become born again, our heart or human spirit is recreated into a brand-new person. Faster than the blink of an eye, the power of God removes the old sin nature and puts within us a spirit of righteousness and holiness (see Ephesians 4:24).

However, soulish things change through a process and over a period of time. This is why we need to hear the same information over and over again. The mind is not instantly recreated like our heart when we are born again. Our mind is designed to be renewed day by day until our thought patterns reflect the plan of God for our life and the level of life God wants us to live.

TAKING CARE OF THE MIND

So it's important for us to learn how to take care of our mind. Our mind is sensitive to every piece of information it receives, either from the spirit realm or from this physical world. We can't put trashy, trivial material in our mind on a regular basis and then be able to think great, positive, and powerful thoughts during a crisis or when under pressure.

When we eat something that causes food poisoning, the pain in our stomach quickly lets us know about it. Our mind is much more vulnerable because thoughts and ideas, whether true or not, can be fed into it without sensing any change. What we initially put into our mind does not immediately show up in our thinking or attitudes. But if we look at or listen to certain things long enough, we will develop corresponding attitudes in our soul that effect everything else in our life.

Negative, unforgiving, hateful attitudes are detrimental to our well-being and contribute to having a toxic or poisoned outlook on life and people. For example, doubtful thoughts can develop into an attitude that will poison our soul. It will eat away at our confidence and our courage. A person who doubts themselves will sabotage their progress in life just like shooting themselves in the foot with a gun hinders their ability to walk. Doubt will undermine our ability to trust in God, His Word, and in ourselves—and thus a roadblock is thrown in the way of our progress and achievements.

Discovering what God's Word says about us can help us choose what thoughts we should think about ourselves and change our self-esteem to improve the way we see ourselves. We must learn to believe in ourselves—that we are who God created us to be and that we can fulfill His will. If we don't believe in ourselves, nobody else will either. The thoughts we think about ourselves will eventually determine the level of our self-esteem and the value we place on ourselves. Our thoughts can be our best support or our worst hindrances.

WHAT DWELLS IN OUR MIND AFFECTS US

Some people freely and openly hate other people. But this has a very detrimental effect on our mind—narrowing our thought processes and jamming our brainwaves with unproductive or harmful ideas. Allowing things like hatred, fear, bitterness, and unforgiveness in our lives will poison our mind. These kinds of things cause our thinking to go into a toxic downward spiral morally, socially, and in other ways.

There is no doubt that when negative and harmful things happen to us, it greatly affects our mind and our emotions. When a loved one passes away, sorrow threatens to overpower us mentally and emotionally. However, sorrow is a wound that will heal with time, unless it gets infected with things like bitterness, self-pity, or unforgiveness. Each person will at some point in their lifetime experience wounds in their soul. However, it is the choice of each person whether they allow their soul to become poisoned with thoughts and attitudes as a result of those wounds, or they accept the healing God has for them and move on to accomplish greater things in life.

We must not allow our minds to continually dwell on the past. The more we think of the unfairness of what has happened, the injustices we've suffered, or the opportunities we've missed, the stronger the chains of the past will become. Often people continue to poison their minds and are held captive by holding on to the memories of negative things that happened in the past.

When people refuse to forgive others for what they did, they are holding on to what has happened, and they end up reliving it every time it comes to their mind. We must learn to let go of what happened in the past. The Bible tells us to forget about these things (see Philippians 3:13). It is amazing how free we are to receive God's abundant, merciful, compassionate care when we release what has happened to us and give it to God.

GET RID OF THE TRASH

We must not allow people to dump their trashy thoughts on us. We are not a landfill where people are allowed to dump their garbage. We must limit our time around people who want to dump their toxic, harmful words and opinions on us. The truth is, we can't move ahead unless we choose our mental diet carefully, for it will eventually yield a harvest.

If we are careful about the correct ingredients being on the labels of the food we eat, we should be much more careful about the ingredients we allow to enter into our mind. When we treat our mind more carelessly than we do our stomach, eventually this will contribute to the overall condition of our soul. This means that we should realize the importance of every thought and its potential to help us reach our goals or hinder us in some way.

Many things around us influence what we think in our minds. Certain things can trigger memories of hurtful, negative experiences in the past. So we must be on our guard, choosing to stay away from things that have a negative impact upon us, such as certain reading materials, harmful television or radio programs, negative and toxic people, and places with negative or unsafe environments. Listening to the wrong information only creates more obstacles in our mind for us to overcome.

We must censor what we watch and listen to, because our eyes and ears are always gathering information to send to our mind. There are negative, toxic things all around us, such as someone complaining or putting us down. These things will influence our thinking and hinder our progress. These things knock on the door of our mind every day. We can't help if someone knocks, but we can decide if we'll open the door and allow them to deposit their harmful things in our minds.

OVERCOME NEGATIVE THOUGHT PATTERNS

When we find our mind has already been poisoned, there is still hope. Sometimes people dump their trashy opinions and words on the doorstep of our mind before we can close the door. The good news is that we can still rid our mind of those poisonous thoughts. To get rid of someone's negative, harmful comments requires multiple inputs of positive, supportive thoughts. It takes a number of correct inputs to nullify the effects of one incorrect input into our mind.

We can overcome negative thought patterns by maintaining a controlled and regular diet of correct material into our mind and then letting the power of the Holy Spirit change our thinking. That is why we need to renew our mind by the daily "washing of the word" (see Ephesians 5:26). God said it is possible for each one of us to be *"transformed by the renewing of your mind, that you may prove what is that good and acceptable and perfect will of God"* (Romans 12:2 NKJV).

CHAPTER 4

CHANGING OUR MIND

"Our greatest support and our worst hindrances are the thoughts we choose to entertain about ourselves."

I once visited with a young man who talked of being a major league baseball pitcher. He was able throw a fast ball in the 90 miles per hour range, and his control was fairly good. At one point he contacted a major league team, and they agreed to take a look at him. He had practiced diligently to prepare for his upcoming tryout with the team. But just weeks before his tryout date, he sustained a shoulder injury and was unable to perform on his tryout date. When I asked this young man if he would fully recover from the injury, he replied the doctors said he would. But he went on to say that he believed no major league baseball team would give him a chance after having had that kind of injury. Even though I encouraged him to ask other teams for a chance to try out, he told me that he had given up and resigned himself to working a job at a local store.

TOO MANY UNREALIZED DREAMS

I've run across a number of good, solid, capable people who have resigned themselves to their life being the way it is with no hope of change. Often these people can tell you what they wanted to be or dreamed about being in life. They started out with great aspirations about who they wanted to be and the things they wanted to accomplish in life.

But when they're asked if they accomplished their dreams, with a sad look they proceed to tell why they couldn't get it done. They offer multiple reasons why it is now too late to achieve those dreams. Many of them will refer to personal circumstances, economic or political conditions, social viewpoints, family upbringing, or religious beliefs as reasons why they didn't do better in life. They didn't know to look to God's promises to keep their hope alive until they had the opportunity to live their dream.

Many of them got busy working a job year after year to provide for their family. Others lost their ability to believe they could do anything other than what they're doing. Making too many mistakes, missing an opportunity, or having to go to work to pay bills are real issues that people face in life. It is true that our mistakes, missed opportunities, repeated failures, accidents, or being ripped off by someone may temporarily kick our dreams and goals off the playing field of life. But we have to realize that doesn't have to be the end of our story. If we'll follow God, He is able help us recover and create circumstances that give us another chance at our dreams or to do something even better.

GOD HAS GIVEN US THE KEY

God has told us in His Word what to do if we want to experience our dreams and fulfill God's plan for our lives. The world may give us every reason why it isn't possible to obey God or achieve what we feel is our assignment in life. However, what God told us to do is very simple: *"And do not be conformed to this world, but be transformed by the renewing of your mind, that you may prove what is that good and acceptable and perfect will of God"* (Romans 12:2 NKJV).

The idea presented here is that when we renew our mind with God's Word, a transformation will happen inside of us. This transformation is necessary so we have the right outlook in life as we negotiate the circumstances and situations of life until we reach our goal. Changing our mind to think the way God wants us to think will position us to achieve God's plans for our lives.

Our society has given us an interesting but somewhat misleading expectation about the word *transformation*. Some of the movies today depict superheroes who give us a modern-day image of the word *transform*, by which a mere human can be instantly transformed into a mighty superhero wearing a bodysuit with a cape who masters every circumstance and every foe. We all love the idea of our lives being suddenly transformed so that we could live the life we always wanted to live.

Our world today focuses on having everything as instant as possible. Fast food restaurants, convenience stores, instant cash machines, and multi-lane highways all affirm our "instant mentality." For some people, a major crisis occurs when they can't find the remote control for the television, they can't instantly flip to the channel they want to watch, or they can't set it up to watch multiple channels at one time. But the word *transform* indicates a very specific way in which change occurs in the human soul.

TRANSFORMING OUR SOUL

The word for "transformed" in the Greek is the word *metamorphoo*. It's the same Greek word from which our English word *metamorphosis* is derived. It means to undergo a complete change of form or the process of constructing something into a different shape. Biologically, it indicates a process of change over a period of time, as in the process whereby a caterpillar changes into a cocoon and then into a beautiful butterfly. It takes time for this change to take place. It doesn't happen instantaneously, or even overnight.

This is what happens as we start the renewal process of daily reading the Word of God and letting the Holy Spirit do His work in us. When we become a Christian, our mind is like an ugly caterpillar, predominantly filled with the ugly, carnal thoughts of the world and the flesh. Our mind must go through the process of metamorphosis to become a beautiful butterfly that expresses the beauty and purposes of God found in Scripture. We are then capable of going to the high places in life for which we were created. However, this takes time to happen.

Soulish things change through a process over a period of time, which is why we need to hear the same information over and over again. We need the continual *"washing of water by the word"* (Ephesians 5:26 NKJV) to cleanse our mind from harmful thoughts, ideas, imaginations, and memories. This brings out the value of daily devotions in the Word of God, which cleanse our minds of the things of the world and fill our minds with thoughts of God's Word. Continually thinking thoughts from the Word of God allows us to rise up into new realms of living we've never before experienced.

DEAL WITH THE OLD AND THE NEW

Early in the ministry of Jeremiah, God reveals a process to him: *"See, I have this day set you over the nations and over the kingdoms, to root out and to pull down, to destroy and to throw down, to build and to plant"* (Jeremiah 1:10 NKJV). Both negative and positive events take place to complete the process of change so that we can move to higher realms of living. Notice the things that are mentioned: 1) to root out, 2) to pull down, 3) to destroy, 4) to throw down, 5) to plant, and 6) to build.

Many people play "dodgeball" with potentially negative situations to try to maintain peace of mind. They try to ignore their problems or will not admit to the negative conditions that may be present. But often it is necessary to root out, pull down, destroy, and throw down things from within of our soul as well as successfully planting and building the things we want there. We cannot move up to new levels of life with old things hanging on us. If we attempt to do so, these old things will undermine our progress, and when we least expect it (when the pressure is the greatest and the moment is most crucial) these old things often cause us to stumble and fall.

REMODELING THE SOUL

A prosperous soul is one in which negative and harmful ideas, thoughts, imaginations, and attitudes are being rooted out, pulled down, destroyed, and thrown down. Then new ideas and thoughts, which are in agreement with the Word of God and the level of life you want to live, are planted and built into the soul.

If we decide to remodel our kitchen, there is a tearing out phase that must take place before the new fixtures can be installed. We must first take out all the old fixtures and the old floor covering.

We must check the framing and foundation and repair it if needed to make sure all of it is solid and stable. Nothing positive seems to be happening in the initial "destruction" stage, unless we keep in mind that we are doing all of this to make room for the new things desired in the kitchen.

By the same token, tearing out the old things is not enough either. There comes a time to install the new floor covering, paint the walls, and install the cabinets and other fixtures. When the kitchen remodeling project is finally finished, we will have gone through both the "tearing out" and the "building" stages. The remodeling was accomplished through the process of taking out the old and replacing it with the new.

PUTTING OFF AND PUTTING ON

The apostle Paul talks about this in his letters to the Ephesian and Colossian churches. He shows the process whereby a person is changed so they can become the person God wants them to be in life.

> *If indeed you have heard Him and have been taught by Him, as the truth is in Jesus: that you put off, concerning your former conduct, the old man which grows corrupt according to the deceitful lusts, and be renewed in the spirit of your mind, and that you put on the new man which was created according to God, in true righteousness and holiness* (Ephesians 4:21-24 NKJV).

> *But now you yourselves are to put off all these: anger, wrath, malice, blasphemy, filthy language out of your mouth. Do not lie to one another, since you have put off the old man with his deeds, and have put on the new man*

who is renewed in knowledge according to the image of
Him who created him (Colossians 3:8-10 NKJV).

Paul instructed believers to put off the old man and put on the new man. Both are necessary if we're going to get where God wants us to be. Once we're born again, believing what God's Word tells us will cause change to take place in our mind. Embracing both what the Word of God tells us *not to be* and what it tells us *to be* enables us to change the attitudes of our mind.

It may not be fun to identify old thoughts and attitudes and judge them as unacceptable by what the Word tells us. However, we can get through this part of the process by keeping in mind that this is necessary so we can implement the Word of God for a new way of thinking that God wants us to have.

REPLACE THE OLD WITH THE NEW

Sometimes people read something like this and think they can or should reach a level of life that is free of all pain and trouble. However, the Bible tells us that in this life we will face trouble and adversity. Throughout our lives, God desires for us to progress in His will by continually putting off the old, negative, carnal thoughts and putting into our mind thoughts that are in line with God's promises and His will. Again, this is a continual process that takes place over a period of time.

It's not enough to identify and concentrate on stopping a particular habit or action. After we have identified the problem, we must then concentrate on the answer. When we concentrate only on what we want to get rid of, we focus so much on what we don't want that we often end up doing what we were trying to get rid of. The key is exchanging what we don't want with what we want to start doing.

What many people don't realize is that denial by itself will often lead to compulsion. This explains why many people on a diet are not successful in losing weight. They are concentrating too much on what they can't have (food) or want to rid themselves of (their weight). Not only do they have to identify what they want to get rid of but they also must focus on what they want to obtain (better health, more energy, better appearance, more confidence, etc.).

Simply denying yourself of something is not enough. Resisting something negative or harmful is not enough. We must also focus on replacing what we're trying to get out of our life with what we want to put into our life.

THE HOLY SPIRIT WILL HELP US

> *But all of us who are Christians have no veils on our faces, but reflect like mirrors the glory of the Lord. We are transfigured by the Spirit of the Lord in ever-increasing splendour into his own image* (2 Corinthians 3:18 PNT).

The word *transfigured* is from the same Greek word *metamorphoo* that is translated as "transformed" in Romans 12:2. This verse reveals that the Holy Spirit has a major role in the transformation of our mind. He works in us to bring change while we're renewing our minds according to God's Word. His convicting power convinces us that we must continually embrace the truth of God's Word. He will teach us concerning the Word of God. He will lead us into the truth that we need to hear so we can become the person God designed us to be. He illuminates our understanding of the Word of God so we can see who God wants us to be and what He wants us to accomplish in life.

We must pay the price to get into the place where the presence and glory of the Spirit manifests, whether that is in our personal lives or as a part of a church congregation. Satan resists us as we endeavor to be faithful in seeking the Lord in Word and prayer. Our flesh lags in interest to conform to God's will. The cares of the world and the challenges of life want to keep us too busy to spend time with God. However, the price we pay is small compared to the reward we receive of living life at the level God intended for us.

COOPERATE WITH THE HOLY SPIRIT

Personal devotion time is necessary so the Holy Spirit can give us understanding of the Word, whisper encouragement to our hearts and minds, and transform us more and more into the image of Christ. We must realize the Holy Spirit is busy working in us while we read the Word of God. It is impossible to stay the same if we regularly read the Word with a believing heart and a receptive mind. Every time we read the Word of God, we are changed. We may not be able to measure the difference from one day to the next, but as we daily read the Word, the Holy Spirit is changing us from the inside out.

Times of corporate worship are absolutely necessary as well. By design we are social creatures who function best if we regularly join with others of like faith to worship God. The Holy Spirit will work in us during these times of corporate worship when His presence and glory is manifested.

WHAT HAPPENS IN CHURCH

It is during those times of worship when we become more receptive and yield more easily to what God wants to do in our lives. In that atmosphere of the presence and glory of the Holy Spirit, inner changes can take place in our lives that couldn't happen any other way. We won't become all God wants us to be unless we're willing to be an active part of a local congregation where the presence and glory of God is being manifested and let Him have His way.

In this atmosphere of the Spirit of Glory, satan cannot readily withstand us, and our mind will yield more quickly to God's thoughts. Somehow, in the midst of the glory of God, our natural human thoughts don't matter as much anymore, earthly things become less important, and we come to the place where we want to think more and more on the thoughts of God.

So we must do what we have to in order to get into a place where God's presence and glory is being manifested. The people who take time to prepare and purposely arrange their schedules so they can regularly experience the presence and power of the Holy Spirit, both personally as well as corporately, are the ones who experience the changes that God is speaking of in 2 Corinthians 3:18. As we purpose in our hearts to spend time with God in worship, in His Word, in prayer, and with God's people, then God can manifest His glory and power to bring about the changes we need in our life.

TRANSFORMATION IS ONGOING

By now we can see that renewing our mind is not a one-time effort. It is a daily endeavor that leads to continual change within us. Some things in life have to be done repeatedly in order to gain the benefit of it. We can mow and trim our lawn ever so well until it looks perfect. Yet in a little while we must do it again. It is the same way with our mind; it does not stay renewed any more than our lawns stay mowed!

Look at what the apostle Paul said: *"Who delivered us from so great a death, and does deliver us; in whom we trust that He will still deliver us"* (2 Corinthians 1:10 NKJV). Notice in this verse that three different phases are mentioned: "delivered" (past tense), "does deliver" (present tense), and "will still deliver" (future tense).

When we were born again we were delivered (past tense) in our spirit. God is also daily delivering (present tense) our soul as it is renewed by the Word of God. It is an ongoing process that is presently happening. And like Paul, we are to trust that God will still deliver (future tense) our bodies in the Rapture when Christ returns for the Church, which is His Body.

We must realize that the process of changing the soul is ongoing. It is continuous, no matter how far we've come. This is how the soul functions. This explains why a person can have a spiritual experience on Sunday and then act carnal on Monday. The process of changing the soul is not yet complete. Some people receive from God one day and act very immature the next day because their minds are not fully transformed by the Word of God.

THE PROCESS OF MIND RENEWAL

Even those who are committed to Christ and are dedicated to the work of Christ may experience varied feelings and conflicting thoughts. While God doesn't intend for us to live our life guided by our feelings, it is not abnormal to have feelings that vary. But to maintain the victorious life God wants us to have, we must evaluate every thought and feeling and bring them into subjection to God's Word.

Sometimes people will do things to us that bring out the "unrenewed" part of our mind. Perhaps someone makes a snide remark or does something stupid while driving in front of us, or someone gets the item we wanted on the shelf at the store, or our extra efforts to complete the project we had been working on aren't recognized or valued. Different things cause people to react in a carnal way.

We know we are not to yield to that part of our soul. Thank God for the Holy Spirit—our Helper—who dwells in our born-again spirit or heart on the inside of us! He will remind us to think and walk according to the Word of God while we're in the process of renewing our mind. The good news is that while we are renewing our mind, God will strengthen us, keep us, and sustain us by the Holy Spirit.

GOD CONTINUALLY WORKS IN US

Just remember that what God has started, He will also finish. God does not give up on us, so we should not give up on ourselves either. The following Scriptures show that God will keep helping us to renew our mind with His Word and move us up into new levels of life. We should look at verses like these until we're confident that God is working in our lives, whether or not we are currently seeing or hearing anything from Him at the moment:

> *The Lord will perfect that which concerns me; Your mercy, O Lord, endures forever; do not forsake the works of Your hands* (Psalm 138:8 NKJV).

> *Being confident of this very thing, that He who has begun a good work in you will complete it until the day of Jesus Christ* (Philippians 1:6 NKJV).

> *Looking unto Jesus, the author and finisher of our faith* (Hebrews 12:2 NKJV).

CHAPTER 5

CONTROLLING OUR THOUGHTS

"Our world has become the way it is by the habitual thoughts we have entertained, and it cannot be changed until we change what we think."

During my growing up years, I attended a traditional church where I got the idea that God was a hard taskmaster, and He was only pleased if you did a lot of good deeds, which seemed impossible to do all the time. The ministers mostly looked stern and unapproachable, and the church services had a somber, pious tone. This led me to think that God wouldn't love or accept me even if I did come to Him. I thought surely God would find something wrong with me, so I tried to stay as far away from God as possible.

However, through a series of divinely arranged events as a young man I did turn my life over to God. But the old thoughts and ideas I previously had about God still tried to influence my thinking.

It was only by renewing my mind to God's Word that gradually I began to see the truth about God and how He loved and accepted me, how He was for me and not against me, and that He would never give up on me.

There are things all around us that will influence our thinking if we allow them. Some people know how to use certain methods and words to manipulate our thinking and cause our thoughts to go in certain directions. Our mind constantly gathers information through our five physical senses, which form ideas and viewpoints in our mind by which we live our lives. If we are able to recognize the things that will potentially influence our thought life, then we can put safeguards in place and minimize the harmful influences around us and also receive godly, positive, supportive information that will affect us in a positive safe way.

IDENTIFY WHAT INFLUENCES OUR SOUL

> *Don't let the world around you squeeze you into its own mould, but let God re-mould your minds from within, so that you may prove in practice that the plan of God for you is good, meets all his demands and moves towards the goal of true maturity* (Romans 12:2 PNT).

Things that influence our thought life in a negative, harmful way can limit what we will be, what we do, and where we live. Likewise, the things that affect our thoughts in a positive safe way can release us into the full potential of what we can be and enable us to move up in life. We must learn to use these influences for our benefit so we can break into new realms of living and achievement. These things may seem superficial, but they have the ability to affect our thoughts and shape the very core of our soul.

The influences in this world that affect our thought life can mostly be put in four categories. They consist of 1) our diet, 2) our friends, 3) our environment, and 4) our words. These four categories influence our five physical senses, which in turn feed information to our soul. As we learn how to control the influence of each of these areas, we will grow in our Christian walk and be more successful in doing what God wants us to do. We will be able to focus better on moving forward into the level of life that God has promised to us. Let's look at each one of these categories to see how they impact our thinking.

#1: OUR DIET!

Nobody likes to go on a diet, but people do it for the benefit it brings them. They do it to be physically fit, become healthy, or improve their appearance. Just as we eat the right kind of physical food, we must also maintain a diet of the right kind of spiritual and mental material if we want to move ahead in life. This is possibly the greatest influence upon our soul. We can't rise higher than the level of information that is put in our minds. The books we read will make the person we are even more than the food we eat.

We can also control our spiritual and mental intake by choosing who we watch and listen to on television, radio, or the Internet. We should ask questions like:

1. "Does this have the same beliefs and values I have?"

2. "Is this promoting the goals and performance level I want to achieve?"

3. "Will this help me move up where God wants me to be in life?"

Having a spiritual and mental diet of books, audio and video products, and things that we can control will empower us to rise to new levels in life.

There is great value in listening to the sermons and teachings of men and women of God who have achieved great things. We can also be inspired as we read biographies of great achievers. Knowing what others have achieved will lift us up to a new level of thinking, vision, and living. It will also help us believe that it is possible for us to achieve our God-given dreams.

Choose the Voices You Listen To

First Corinthians 14:10 (KJV) tells us, *"There are, it may be, so many kinds of voices in the world, and none of them is without signification."* The apostle Paul talks specifically of the need to understand the different languages of the world in order to benefit from them. In a broader sense, this verse shows that every voice, no matter what language it speaks, contends for people's attention to influence their thoughts. Before we embrace what someone tells us, we must ask ourselves, "Is this a positive, helpful message that is in agreement with the Word of God, and does its message reflect where we know God wants us to be?"

Today we can listen to many ministers on Christian radio, television, the Internet, and in local congregations. Each one emphasizes something specifically in their preaching. Collectively they say many different things, some even opposing others. If we continually listen to every minister we have access to, we'll hear and see many different things. This creates potential for confusion in our thinking. This is why we should attend a Bible-believing church on a regular and consistent basis that has a minister who

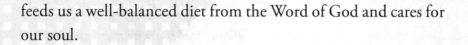

feeds us a well-balanced diet from the Word of God and cares for our soul.

Maintain a Steady Diet

A steady diet of God's Word causes new thoughts to gain prominence in our thinking. We must continually read, hear, and look at materials that help us think the right thoughts so we can believe our needs will be met, overcome temptations and problems, and accomplish our goals in life.

Overcoming great needs or difficulties involves our thought life to be continually focused on the possibilities and solutions available to us. Sometimes we must narrow or intensify our focus—looking and listening consistently to the right material for a period of time, which can accelerate change in our soul, eliminate confusion, and influence our thought life positively so we can receive what we need and accomplish certain things in life.

#2: OUR FRIENDS

Some people don't realize how much influence their friends have on them. People usually decide who their friends are by whoever is friendly to them. Most people don't ask or pay any attention to the beliefs and values of the people they have for friends. But the Word of God tells us to choose our friends carefully because they will either help or hinder us in following God's will for our lives, in reaching our goals, and living our dreams. Look at these verses:

> *The righteous should choose his friends carefully, for the way of the wicked leads them astray* (Proverbs 12:26 NKJV).

Do not enter the path of the wicked, and do not walk in the way of evil. Avoid it, do not travel on it; turn away from it and pass on. For they do not sleep unless they have done evil; and their sleep is taken away unless they make someone fall (Proverbs 4:14-16 NKJV).

Do not be deceived: "Evil company corrupts good habits" (1 Corinthians 15:33 NKJV).

Decide Who to Spend Time With

Someone pointed out that all relationships can be put in four categories—those who add to and multiply into our life, or those who subtract or divide from our life. We must identify each relationship truthfully and honestly. Most people form their relationships with those who have similar negative issues or with those who have common interests. When we choose friends based on shared problems, we're building on a negative foundation that can lead to more problems and unhealthy, unsafe relationships. These relationships are usually temporary. But relationships built on common interests can help us form lasting, healthy relationships that enable us to reach our full potential and live the life God planned for us.

The people we closely associate with on a regular basis will have great influence on the outcome of our life. We must learn not to spend time with people who put down our dreams and ambitions. Those who think small thoughts tend to pull us down to their level. Those with great thoughts often have a positive effect on us, making us feel we can do something great too. So we must decide who we will include in our inner circle and who will be in our outer circle of acquaintances.

Identify Our Inner and Outer Circles

Most of us have both an inner circle of friends and an outer circle of acquaintances. Our inner circle of friends should consist of those who hold the same beliefs and values that we do. They should be those who are able to help each other climb higher in life, support each other, believe in one another, and are loyal to one another. Our outer circle of friends will be those who are friendly toward us, but they do not necessarily hold the same values and beliefs that we do. In other words, if we followed them, they would not lead in the direction we want to go.

Jesus illustrated this in His earthly ministry. There were seventy people who were acquainted with Jesus well enough to help Him in His ministry, but they weren't named in Scripture. Jesus also had twelve disciples, or followers, who were associated with Him so closely that they became His ministry team, and they were mentioned by name in Scripture. Also, within the twelve disciples Jesus chose only three disciples, Peter, James, and John, with whom He shared His special moments. These moments included the time when Jesus raised Jairus' daughter from the dead (Mark 5:37), the transfiguration of Jesus on the mountain (Mark 9:2), and when Jesus was in the Garden of Gethsemane (Mark 14:32-33). Even beyond that, Jesus entrusted His mother only to John and not to the rest of His disciples.

Jesus Chose the Ones Closest to Him

Jesus loved everyone equally, and He willingly helped everyone who wanted His help. As Jesus looked at the multitude of people, He was moved with compassion for them. However, He never spent time with the multitudes unless it was to help them in some way. The people whom Jesus allowed to be close to Him, with the exception of Judas Iscariot, consisted of those who had the same values and beliefs He had.

The influence of God the Father lifted Jesus above the limitations of other people's thinking until He was able to say, do, and accomplish His Father's will. This shows us that spending time with the right people can eventually help us arrive at the right place to do the right things. So Jesus spending quality time in prayer with the right Person—God the Father—while He was here on earth was a major factor that helped Him fulfill His mission and ascend to a place of honor at the right hand of God the Father for eternity.

Don't Burn Bridges

The time may come when one of our close friends no longer exhibits the same beliefs and values as they once did, and they actually begin to negatively influence our relationship. When that happens, we may find a debate going on in our mind about what to do. Do we end the relationship? Or do we just overlook it and act like it doesn't matter? The truth is, we may not have to do either one.

When a person close to us no longer supports us or shares common beliefs, we can gradually move them from our inner circle of associates to our outer circle of acquaintances. Moving that person to our outer circle can be done by not initiating contact with them but responding graciously to them when they contact us, limiting the time we spend with them but being willing to help them if we can, and by carefully evaluating what they have to say. The reason we don't want to burn the relationship is so we can leave the door open to help them if the opportunity arises. And we don't know when we might need their help. The goal is to avoid unnecessary conflict and yet choose wisely who we will have as our close friends. The apostle Paul tells us, *"If it is possible, as much as depends on you, live peaceably with all men"* (Romans 12:18 NKJV).

The Normal Process of Life

It is normal for some people in our inner circle to no longer have the same goals and interests as we progress in the plan God has for our life. God didn't call all of us to do the same things or go to the same destination. Also, some people don't grow at the same pace we're growing. So we have to let them progress at their chosen pace while we continue at the right pace for us in the direction God wants us to go.

Most likely we'll have a few people who are our friends for a long time, and even for a lifetime. But we must also realize that we cannot take everybody with us on the path God has called us to go. Not all our friends are called to go that way. We must gravitate toward and spend most of our time with those who are going in a similar direction to the one we're going. We must love everyone, but we must also limit our close friends to those who have the same values and beliefs that we do.

#3: OUR ENVIRONMENT

Our environment includes many things, such as our surroundings, circumstances, habitats, and places we habitually go. It also includes where many of our experiences in life take place. Where we live and the places we go all have a unique environment. Each environment creates an atmosphere that is either uplifting or depressing to us. Environment is often the silent invisible factor that influences most people's thinking far more than they realize.

Most of us habitually go to the same places during our daily routine. These places make up "our world" and often the environment in these places influences our decisions, helps form our ideas of what we think is possible, and helps us determine what is acceptable or even what we can afford to buy. We can walk into one place and the atmosphere may feel yucky and cheap, and we can't wait to get out of there. In other places, the atmosphere inspires us and makes us believe that great things are possible.

In some work places, the hectic environment with high output demands on employees can create an atmosphere that causes undue stress and agitation and drains creative and organizational skills. On the other hand, a beautiful nature setting can bring a peaceful atmosphere that soothes our soul and restores our thought processes to the level of our full potential.

The world around us often endeavors to conform our thinking to the environment or surroundings we're in. Its influence works on the level of our expectations, motivations, values, moral standards, and even what we believe. The economic condition of our nation wants to influence our thinking. The news media influences our environment by the news it shares. Many in the world focus all their efforts on food, clothing, and shelter, creating an environment which predominantly thinks:

- ▶ "Survival is the name of the game."
- ▶ "We going to get our share before others get it."
- ▶ "Let's get all we can before it's all gone."

Choose a Positive Atmosphere

As believers, we are to seek God who promised to provide all things for us. Seeking God in a godly environment apart from the influence of the world enables us to raise our expectations and place our trust in Him to provide for us. This keeps our financial limitations from being determined by only salary or by the economy in our community. Instead, it allows us to expect God to be our source and continually provide for us, even beyond our natural environment.

The right kind of atmosphere in our homes, churches, and workplaces can inspire us to find solutions and discover creative ways to accomplish things. But the wrong kind of atmosphere will restrict or limit our expectancy of what can be done, causing us to ask, "How do you ever expect me to do that?" instead of confidently saying, "I believe we can we do it!"

Our Church Does Matter

A major avenue by which Christian people's thinking is influenced is by their religious environment. What a church believes and teaches will shape the environment in the church congregation and influence people's thoughts and beliefs. In some churches, they teach that God does not care about our circumstances or conditions—that He is not directly involved in the daily affairs of humankind. This diminishes people's expectation that God can or will help them in their situation.

Some churches teach that God will only supply our needs but not our wants. Consequently, when things are needed such as building repairs, furnishings, supplies, or supporting missionaries, their conversations and decision-making processes are often dominated by comments such as, "Well, we can't afford that," or "We can't do that because we don't have very much." These comments reveal the level of their expectation, what they can believe God will do for them, and thus limit what they attempt to do.

These activities and words contribute to the atmosphere in that church building, and whenever new people step into that church environment, unconsciously their thinking is influenced by it. Habitually being in this type of environment influences people's thinking, often without them realizing it. What they repeatedly hear in church will eventually form a mental picture of who God is and what He will or will not do.

This is one reason many Christian people are barely getting by—they have repeatedly heard that God is not interested in their daily wants or desires, and therefore they think they must be content with whatever their circumstances are. They are operating in the perimeters formed by the world around them instead of the possibilities revealed in the promises of God's Word.

This shows the value of finding and regularly attending a Bible-believing church where God's Word is taught. When the truth of God's Word is taught, people are set free to walk in God's will and they can expect God to watch over them and provide for them.

#4: OUR WORDS

Words surround us on every side. We hear them, see them, read them, and speak them. Many words are containers of positive things like hope, love, victory, freedom, and possibility. Words can also contain negative things like despair, hate, defeat, failure, shame, and condemnation. Words shape our thinking, our expectations, our actions, and our destinies, for they are some of the most powerful things in the world.

Indeed, the Bible tells us the visible worlds—our planet and the universe—were created by the spoken Word of God (Genesis 1; Hebrews 11:3). Jesus Himself said that by our words we are justified or condemned (Matthew 12:37). He also said that if we believe the words we speak, we will eventually have what we say (Mark 11:23).

Many people don't realize how much their own words or the words of other people they listen to will influence their thinking. Nor do they think about how their own words influence their thought life. Negative, condemning words can cause our thoughts to go into a downward spiral and, left unchecked, leave us in a depressed state of mind. The world is full of people who freely hand out criticism, put-downs, and hateful opinions. They freely spew their toxic rhetoric to anyone who will listen. Of course, we must keep in mind that our spiritual enemy satan influences people in this world to attack others and drag them down until they can't reach their God-given destiny.

Words Can Hurt or Help Us

Words are powerful; they're capable of either tearing down or building up a person. Years may have passed since harmful, negative words were spoken to a person, but often the impact of those words is still evident in the way that person thinks. The apostle Paul wrote, *"Don't use bad language. Say only what is good and helpful to those you are talking to, and what will give them a blessing"* (Ephesians 4:29 TLB).

I heard of a little second grade boy who got in trouble one day at school. That evening his father got very angry and informed him that he could no longer trust him. The father's words cut deep in the soul of that little boy, and from then on those words influenced his thinking and how he viewed himself in life. It hindered his efforts to please his father or to do his best in school. After the young boy became a teenager, what that father said to him in the second grade was still a major influence in their relationship.

Most of us can remember when someone's words, either positive or negative, shaped our thoughts from that time on. What someone says to us can make a great impact upon our thinking, especially if it came from someone we looked up to. It often sets the bar for our level of expectation in life, affects the level of confidence we display, and determines our conduct in relationships. Certain thought processes are developed within us, either good or bad, as a result of information that someone else shares with us. Constant affirmation from others of who we are and what we can do is of great value. This will increase our ability to perform, help us to discover our full potential in life, and raise our expectancy to win in life.

The Power of Affirmation

I heard of another young man who had experienced some difficulties in ministry that ended in him relocating to another city. There he met a pastor who expressed interest in him and allowed him to become involved in his church. The young man thought the pastor ought to know how things had gone previously, and he began to tell him about the difficulties he had gone through.

The pastor stopped the young man and said to him, "I didn't ask for a history lesson. I'm only interested in who I'm seeing right now." The pastor's affirming words had a major influence on that young man's thinking and enabled him to get free from the condemnation of not being successful in the difficult situation he had previously been in. Later on, that young man experienced much success in ministry.

The good news is that we don't have to sit around waiting for someone to say good things to us. We can influence our own thinking by speaking words that reflect who God made us to be and what we were created to do in life. We can speak words affirming the value that God has placed upon us. Others may not forgive us, but we can remind ourselves that God has provided forgiveness for us.

We can take our future in hand by saying the right words to ourselves. This creates thought processes within us that embrace our God-given future. Speaking something one time has little affect upon our thought life. But if we consistently speak words declaring who the Bible says we are and what we can do, eventually we will find ourselves thinking God's plan for us is possible and we'll rise up to that level.

Power to Make the Right Choices

Having a prosperous soul is a process of renewing our mind to God's Word and controlling our thought life. We can greatly accelerate this process by controlling the input from each of these four areas: 1) our spiritual and mental diet (what we watch, read, and listen to); 2) our close friends (those we habitually hang out with); 3) our environment (atmosphere); and 4) our words (what we say). This will enable us to think and believe that God will help us make the right choices and work mightily in our lives to bring forth His will for us.

CHAPTER 6

THE POWER OF OUR WILL

"Truly great accomplishments don't happen spontaneously—they often happen through a series of small things that someone exercises their will to do."

When I was an Amish boy, our family had no car or truck because of our religious beliefs. On Sunday we drove slowly to church in our horse and buggy. But in my imagination I dreamed of driving a 1964 Chevy Super Sport, with blue metallic exterior and white interior, 327 cubic inch motor with a high-rise manifold, four barrel carburetor, and headers with glass pack mufflers that rumbled as it went down the road. It had a four speed shifter on the floor, and Cragar Super Sport chrome mag wheels and 14 inch wide tires on the back. In my mind I dreamed that someday I would drive a car like that. And years later I did own a 1964 Chevy Super Sport very similar to the one I had repeatedly imagined as a young boy.

Some people walk through life exercising strong willpower to chase after their ambitions and get what they want. Others seem weak and unsure of themselves and don't seem to have a very strong determination to stick with anything. Many look enviously at those who have a strong will, but somehow it doesn't seem to be something they have or know how to get.

CREATED WITH A HUMAN WILL

Exercising our human will is necessary to accomplish very much in life. People from various professions have offered a variety of comments on the human will and how it functions. Yet it seems the operation of our human will is one of the least understood parts within the makeup of a human being.

Some believe the human will is subject to no one, that a person will exercise their will independent of any divine influence or force—that a human is in essence a god to himself. Others on the other end of the spectrum say there is no such thing as a person freely exercising their will, that since everything is predestinated according to the foreknowledge of God, the human will is at all times controlled by the will of God. Yet as is often the case, somewhere between these opposing views we can find a scriptural balance concerning our human will.

THE VALUE OF OUR HUMAN WILL

A number of places in Scripture show us the human will is part of our soul. For our soul to prosper, we must discover how the human will functions and how to align our human will to God's will. When our human will is consecrated and conformed to God's will, we can make great strides in following God and moving up into new realms of God's promises.

> *When He had stopped speaking, He said to Simon, "Launch out into the deep and let down your nets for a catch." But Simon answered and said to Him, "Master, we have toiled all night and caught nothing; nevertheless at Your word I will let down the net." And when they had done this, they caught a great number of fish, and their net was breaking. So they signaled to their partners in the other boat to come and help them. And they came and filled both the boats, so that they began to sink* (Luke 5:4-7 NKJV).

Here we see Peter submitting his will to what Jesus told him to do. Peter had fished all night and caught nothing. Yet when Jesus told Peter to let down his nets, he had to go against the natural wisdom he normally used in fishing and obey what Jesus told him to do. After Peter aligned his human will to God's will, he was greatly rewarded with a large amount of fish.

In the Garden of Gethsemane, Jesus prayed, *"Father, if it is Your will, take this cup away from Me; nevertheless not My will, but Yours, be done"* (Luke 22:42 NKJV). He prayed this same prayer three times, showing that submitting our will to God's will is a continual process. Here in this critical moment, Jesus voluntarily yielded His own will to go to the Cross to die for the sins of all humankind. Without Jesus' submission to His Father's will, He could not have accomplished the plan of redemption for humankind.

But submitting His will to His Father's will enabled Jesus to accomplish the plan of redemption for humankind. This is a powerful example of consecrating and conforming our human will to the will of our heavenly Father, and it provides a pattern of daily consecration in prayer to His will for us.

DEFINING THE HUMAN WILL

The human will can be looked at as a person's ability to control their impulses or instincts. Sometimes a person is referred to as having a strong will or someone who has the capability to control their impulses. Words that describe the human will include *determination*, *choice*, *purpose*, or *inclination*. These words describe a person who exercises their human will, i.e., "He determined or purposed to go to the ball game," or "Of her own choice she went with her friend."

The human will is designed to be in submission, either to God's will or to satan's will. A human being cannot exercise their human will independently from the influence of God's or satan's will. It is always influenced by either one or the other. For example, when a person is disobedient or in rebellion to God, they have in essence submitted their will to the influence of satan's will.

A few years ago, Frank Sinatra sang a song entitled, "I Did It My Way." But the truth is that nobody really lives their life their own way. When someone thinks they did it their own way, they are believing a lie. Either God's will or satan's will influences the human will of every human being to do what they do. Invisible, spiritual forces influence people to exercise their human will in certain ways, often without them being conscious of it happening.

GOD HAS A WILL

> *Thou art worthy, O Lord, to receive glory and honour and power: for thou hast created all things, and for thy pleasure they are and were created* (Revelation 4:11 KJV).

The word *pleasure* in this verse comes from the same Greek word that is also translated elsewhere in the Scriptures as "will." By this we can see that God's will and God's pleasure are connected and operate in agreement. It was the will of God to originally create all things for His pleasure. At the end of the seven days of creation, God looked at all He had made, and His evaluation was that it was very good, or very pleasing to Him (see Genesis 1:31).

After the fall of man in the Garden of Eden when they disobeyed God, Adam's lineage existed in sin and unrighteousness for over 5,000 years. Although the children of Israel were selected by God to be His people, they had not been born again since Jesus hadn't yet provided redemption for all who believe in Him. In the fullness of time, it pleased God to exercise His will to provide redemption for humankind through Jesus Christ and recreate those who believe in Him (see Galatians 4:4).

Therefore, the born-again person is a product of both God's will and pleasure. The apostle John wrote in his gospel:

> But as many as received Him, to them He gave the right to become children of God, to those who believe in His name: who were born, not of blood, nor of the will of the flesh, nor of the will of man, but of God (John 1:12-13 NKJV).

JESUS CAME TO DO THE FATHER'S WILL

Jesus was born, not by man's will, but by the will of God. John 6:38 (NKJV) tells us He lived and ministered by the will of God, *"For I have come down from heaven, not to do My own will, but the will of Him who sent Me."* Also Jesus, in accordance with the will of God the Father, gave Himself for our sins. The apostle Paul tells us that

Christ, *"gave Himself for our sins, that He might deliver us from this present evil age, according to the will of our God and Father"* (Galatians 1:4 NKJV).

God has written His will for humankind in His Word, and these two things cannot be separated. Just as Jesus came in the flesh to reveal the will of the Father, so the written Word also reveals the will of God to us. God is not a man that He should lie, saying one thing in His Word and then using His divine will to do something different. God is faithful to His Word and will do what He has promised in His Word. Abraham received the promise of God after he became fully persuaded that what God had promised, He was also able to perform (see Romans 4:21).

SATAN ALSO HAS A WILL

How you are fallen from heaven, O Lucifer, son of the morning! How you are cut down to the ground, you who weakened the nations! For you have said in your heart: "I will ascend into heaven, I will exalt my throne above the stars of God; I will also sit on the mount of the congregation on the farthest sides of the north; I will ascend above the heights of the clouds, I will be like the Most High" (Isaiah 14:12-14 NKJV).

In these verses, we find what can be called the five "I wills" of satan. Satan made five different statements and each one began with "I will." All five of these statements opposed God and show that satan wanted to take over God's kingdom. By doing this, satan exercised his will against God's will and rebelled against God. However, he did not prevail in what he wanted to do. In the end, God cast satan out of Heaven along with one third of the angels who chose to follow satan. This is the first recorded act of rebellion against God's will in the Bible.

Today, satan is continually trying to influence people to rebel against God's will. People who rebel against God's plan are being influenced, often without realizing it, by satan and his demonic spirits. Those who are exercising their will against God's will have yielded their will to satan's will and are committing iniquity or sin; they are missing the mark of doing God's will and are rebelling against what God wanted for them.

EXAMPLES OF THE HUMAN WILL

Several generations after the flood, Noah's descendants began to build a tower on the plains of Shinar that would reach the heavens, intending to make sure that they had a place to go if God ever sent another flood. They had either forgotten or did not believe that God had promised that He would never again send another flood. God came to see what they were doing, and then He said, *"Indeed the people are one and they all have one language, and this is what they begin to do; now nothing that they propose to do will be withheld from them"* (Genesis 11:6 NKJV).

The Hebrew meaning of the word *propose* in this verse includes the idea of imagining what to do and then exercising the human will to accomplish it. By exercising their will according to their imaginations, these people began to set the direction they intended to go in their lives. God saw that and said nothing on earth can stop them. Imaginations and the human will are connected, and when they operate in agreement, it makes a powerful force to accomplish great and mighty things. For this reason, we must be careful to conform our imaginations and human will to the will of God.

The apostle Paul describes the condition of a person before they receive salvation: *"we all once conducted ourselves in the lusts of our flesh, fulfilling the desires of the flesh and of the mind, and were by nature children of wrath, just as the others"* (Ephesians 2:3 NKJV). Those who have not experienced salvation are *"children of wrath"* who have a lifestyle of following the lust or will of their flesh. Throughout the Word of God, descriptions of the human condition reflect God's nature and character or they depict the activities and character of satan. This reveals that the human will is subject to either godly or satanic influence. While sinners, people did what they thought they wanted to do. But in actuality, by doing things contrary to God's will, they are simply conforming to satan's desires.

TWO REQUIREMENTS FOR A BETTER LIFE

If you are willing and obedient, you shall eat the good of the land (Isaiah 1:19 NKJV).

Here God tells Israel that as a nation they must be both willing and obedient to obey God's commands. This positioned them to experience the blessings God had promised to them. Have you ever met someone who was obedient but grumbled while obeying? Even though they did what they were told, they still had an unwilling attitude. This kept the blessing of God from flowing in their lives. This verse shows that the blessing of God comes after conforming our will to what He said to do and then obeying Him.

It doesn't take long to make the adjustment in our attitude to go from being unwilling to being willing. Sometimes God asks us to do something that doesn't make much sense to our mind. But we must realize that whatever He asks us to do makes perfect sense from His perspective. As we become willing to do God's will, His plan becomes clearer and makes more sense to us. Look at the incident of Jesus telling Peter to launch his boats out into the deep to catch fish after he had labored all night and caught nothing. Here is Peter's response: *"Master, we have toiled all night and caught nothing; nevertheless at Your word I will let down the net"* (Luke 5:5 NKJV).

Peter didn't try to figure out how it would work if he obeyed God. Although he had spent all night fishing and had caught nothing, now Jesus told him to throw his nets in the same place. Here Peter aligned his will to do what Jesus said and reaped great benefits because of it. His willingness and obedience opened the door for him to experience a miraculous supply. Often the supply we need comes after we can align our will to God's Word and then obey Him.

IDENTIFYING STRONG SOULISH DESIRES

Sometimes people have difficulty discerning between the will of God and their own soulish desires. This often happens when they have nurtured strong soulish desires for a long time. Many Christians do not know how to separate strong soulish desires they have cultivated for years (especially while growing up) from the will of God.

If we exercise our will according to these soulish desires and not according to the will of God, our soul may experience negative trauma, turmoil, or sorrow. In the Garden of Eden, Eve listened to the serpent telling her that it was okay for her to eat of the tree of the knowledge of good and evil. As she considered what the serpent had told her, she saw the tree *"was good for food, that it was pleasant to the eyes, and a tree desirable to make one wise"* (Genesis 3:6 NKJV). This created a strong desire within her and she exercised her will to eat of the fruit of the tree. Afterward, God told Eve, *"I will greatly multiply your sorrow and your conception; in pain you shall bring forth children; your desire shall be for your husband, and he shall rule over you"* (Genesis 3:16 NKJV).

THE POWER OF THE HUMAN WILL

There is power in our human will to accomplish things, either according to God's will or against it. This is why we must learn to conform our will to God's will.

I heard of a man who as a child went with his father to a tall building where they took the elevator clear to the top floor. There they entered into a beautiful office with soft carpet and a beautiful wooden desk. Deep in his heart the little boy said to himself that someday he would have an office like that. Over the course of time, the little boy grew up having to deal with various jobs and other issues. Suddenly one day, a business opportunity came his way, and after the final negotiations were done the people who hired him took him to his office. It was almost identical to the one he had seen as a small boy. The human will has the power to create opportunities to bring things to pass.

CONFORMING OUR WILL IS VITAL

As you can see, exercising the power of the human will can cause things to come to pass. Since we could exercise our will against God's will, it is important that we conform our will to God's will. We must take time to seek Him so we can separate our deep-rooted soulish desires from what is actually the will of God.

Unless a person's human will is conformed to God's will, we may open the door to things that God doesn't want for us. If a person goes far enough in this area they may end up manipulating other people to get what they want, regardless of whether it benefits others. This borders on what the Bible calls witchcraft, in which a person forces their human will upon other people against their wishes and without regard for what the will of God may be. Let this be our daily prayer, "Not my will, O God, but Thy will be done."

CHAPTER 7

ALIGNING OUR WILL

"The most important thing an individual can do is obey God's will and pray, 'God, Your will be done.'"

During my growing up years, our family didn't have a lot of material things like other families had in our community. That seemed to bother me more than it did any of my other siblings, and at an early age I set goals to become a businessman and make a lot of money. Consequently, when as a young man I received the call of God to the ministry, I reacted rather negatively. My dream was to be in business, not in the pulpit. I had given my heart to Christ, but unfortunately my mind was still full of my own ideas. I begged God to leave me alone so I could be a businessman, and I promised to support those who did preach the Gospel. However, God did not change His mind, and over a period of time I came to the place of aligning myself to God's plan and accepting His call into ministry. Following God's will has been the best thing I ever did in my entire life.

To know our purpose in life and do God's will is the highest privilege that a person can have. Knowing God's will can free us from the arm-twisting manipulations of the enemy and from the opinions and desires of other people. Aligning our will with God's will and walking in His plan allows us to experience freedom from frustration and have peace of mind. Nothing is more peaceful for a person than to walk in God's will, knowing that God has promised never to leave them nor forsake them (see Hebrews 13:5).

One of David's prayers was, *"Teach me to do Your will, for You are my God; Your Spirit is good. Lead me in the land of uprightness"* (Psalm 143:10). There is no doubt that God is good and He does have ample provision for us; however, this can only be fully experienced by being in His will. This requires us to align our human will to His divine will.

HOW TO ELIMINATE FRUSTRATION

Many people's frustrations are relieved and they gain a sense of purpose when they find out what God's will is and begin to walk in it. God's plan is the ultimate life we could possibly experience here on earth. His plan makes perfect sense to Him, even when it seems impossible or makes no sense to us.

Years ago when I was enrolled in Bible school, in a time of prayer I told God that the job I had was not providing enough income and therefore I was going to get a second job. God responded by clearly telling me to do volunteer work in the church. This made no sense to me whatsoever, and it took several days and several events to persuade me to yield my human will to God's direction. While it made no sense in the natural, doing what God said opened the door for Him to supernaturally supply our needs and get us out of our financial dilemma.

Yielding to God's will represents different things to different people. Some feel that doing God's will means they can have no more fun and enjoyment in life. For others, it represents a radical shift in their lifestyle. I heard of one man who would not yield to God's plan for his life because he was afraid God would call him to serve as a missionary in a foreign land. Some people have earthly possessions that they feel are too much to give up. No matter the reasons a person may have in being reluctant to follow God, they must come to the point of realizing that aligning themselves with God's will is part of having a prosperous soul and the way to the level of life that God intended for us to have.

THE SHAPING OF OUR WILL

The mind and the will are connected and they work together. Throughout the entire length of a person's existence, the mind is always gathering information. Some comes from the five physical senses of the body. Some comes from what others have told us. A person's experiences in life also provide information that is stored in their mind. Satan, our enemy, endeavors to inject his thoughts into our mind. Whatever information is in the mind will provide the basis or reasoning for the human will to resist going one way or moving in a certain direction.

Our early experiences in life are often powerful influences over our human will. Sometimes people struggle with giving up their deep-rooted determination to be the person or have a vocation they had in mind. Often certain things they heard and were taught serve to hold them back from fully consecrating to God's call. It is only through repeatedly devoting and consecrating oneself to God's plan that a person finally reaches the point of fully committing to answer God's plan.

What we have been taught and experienced in our past guides us in what we want to do in life. When God brings us a new plan, a different direction, or a new way of life, we often have to deal with getting free from former thoughts, ideas, and personal ambitions so we can yield to God's plan. That is often more of a process over a period of time than a one-time event. This is why it is important that we daily consecrate our will to God's will as much as we possibly can. And the good news is that the Holy Spirit is with us to create a desire within us to do what God wants us to do.

ALIGNING OUR WILL TO GOD'S WILL

Jesus Christ, the Sinless One, yielding to the divine plan to take the sin of all humanity upon Himself is a game changer for humankind. His alignment to the Father's will now enables those who believe in Him to step into a new life. It is the ultimate story of a person fully aligning their will with God's will. When Jesus knew His time had come to be crucified and suffer for the sins of humankind, He went out into the Garden of Gethsemane to pray.

> *He went a little farther and fell on His face, and prayed, saying, "O My Father, if it is possible, let this cup pass from Me; nevertheless, not as I will, but as You will." ...Again, a second time, He went away and prayed, saying, "O My Father, if this cup cannot pass away from Me unless I drink it, Your will be done." ...So He left them, went away again, and prayed the third time, saying the same words* (Matthew 26:39,42,44 NKJV).

Here we see our Savior fighting the battle of aligning His human will with the will of His Father. It is important to notice that Jesus prayed this prayer of consecration three times. This is the kind of prayer that can we can pray daily to continually align ourselves to the ever-unfolding plan of God for our lives. Today we pray to yield our will in regard to the will of God that we already know and for whatever may come in the future. Tomorrow may bring more understanding of God's will and the need to once again pray *"not as I will, but as You will"* (Matthew 26:39). One minister said after many successful years in ministry that he still prayed this prayer of consecration on a daily basis.

Some people say they don't seem to have any willpower to conform to God's will. They have questions like, "How does a person conform their will completely to God's will?" or "How do we get to the place where we are able to pray the prayer that Jesus prayed in the Garden of Gethsemane and mean it with all our heart?"

Conforming our will so it functions in agreement with God's will is a process of giving up our ideas and goals and embracing the truths and plans of God. This happens little by little, step by step on a daily basis as long as we live on this earth. Often this takes place as we come into the knowledge of God's Word on a particular subject, or it may take place in a time of prayer. Although more principles may be involved, we can clearly identify the following basic principles that help us know where we are in the process of conforming our will.

#1: Know God's Will for You

Look again at one of the prayers of David in which he said, *"Teach me to do Your will, for You are my God; Your Spirit is good. Lead me in the land of uprightness"* (Psalm 143:10 NKJV). David asked

God to teach him His will and how to walk in it, and he indicates his willingness to do the will of God once he knew what it was. We can't act on something we don't know.

Some do not believe we can know the will of God. Others look in various places to discover God's will. They cite places like social media, online information, church creeds, and even opinions of others as to what the will of God might be. However, there is no surer source to know God's will than to read the Word of God. Many of us rightly endeavor to be led by the inner leading of the Holy Spirit for direction. Yet we must recognize that God's leading will always be in agreement with His written Word.

We must keep in mind that God's truth and His will are aligned together, for God does not contradict what He said by what He does. So reading God's Word will reveal His plans to us, and as we consent to the truth of His plans our thoughts will become more conformed to His truth. Our human will either submits or rebels based upon the information received in our mind about an issue. So knowing the Word of God forms a sure basis for conforming our will to fulfill God's will and desires.

#2: Understand the Forces Behind the Human Will

Having strong willpower means our human will has a source of power that it draws from. Power comes into our will because of having the right information in our mind and the right ambitions and motives to do something. This shows a chain effect of things happening when we have strong willpower for something. Everyone has to deal with their motives—the reasons or logic we have in our mind for what we do. For example, if I have information that someone wants to harm me, my motive is to protect myself. Motives create reasons or desires to do certain things, which in turn fuel our will. Motives are based upon the information and experiences that have entered the mind.

We can insure right motives in every situation if we have the Word of God as our primary source. This shows the importance of meditating upon the Word of God. David said, *"Let the words of my mouth and the meditation of my heart be acceptable in Your sight, O Lord, my strength and my Redeemer"* (Psalm 19:14 NKJV). As we meditate on God's Word, it allows the Holy Spirit to work on our inner motives and desires, and we end up wanting to act in agreement with God's will.

#3: Daily Consecrate to God's Will

The process of consecration is necessary until His will becomes our will. This allows the will of God to come to the forefront of our thoughts in any given situation. It takes time, prayer, reflection, and meditation upon God's Word for this to happen. In times of consecration, we lay down our personal ambitions, dreams, and desires and yield ourselves fully to His will. In the end, we will see that the benefits of being aligned to God's will far exceed whatever we had to give up.

To consecrate means to set apart. We must daily consecrate and set ourselves apart to do the will of God. As we do so, we will be able to commit more and more to the will of God. This process will eventually lead us to the place where we are fully set apart and our sole ambition in life is to fulfill the will of God for our life.

> *Epaphras, who is one of you, a bondservant of Christ, greets you, always laboring fervently for you in prayers, that you may stand perfect and complete in all the will of God* (Colossians 4:12 NKJV).

Coming to the place of great consecration requires someone spending time in prayer. Epaphras labored fervently in prayer so that the Colossians would conform to the will of God until they were perfect (or mature) and experienced the will of God completely. During times of consecration, we must accept the fact that without Christ we can do nothing (see John 15:5). We must also acknowledge the truth of Philippians 4:13 (NKJV): *"I can do all things through Christ who strengthens me."* True consecration is entering the place where we desire to do nothing without Christ and are willing to do all things through His strength and power.

#4: Commit Your Will to Do God's Will

Commitment is an act of trust, and therefore most people usually don't reach the place of commitment quickly or easily. We must grow into it. Being committed to the will of God is as important as knowing the will of God. When I was fifteen years old, I had a very dramatic, supernatural experience in which God told me He wanted me to be a minister. At the time, I had very little knowledge of God or His Word and so I discarded what God said to do and followed my own dreams. It was another twelve years before I had enough Bible knowledge to lead me into making a commitment to become the minister God had spoken to me about as a young boy.

So our level of commitment to the will of God determines the value of knowing the will of God. There is little value in having knowledge that we are not committed to walk in or make a part of our life. Being committed to the will of God means being committed to doing what the Word of God says. We cannot separate the will of God from the Word of God because they are one and the same. The way we relate to the Word of God shows the way we will respond to the will of God.

I met a man in a restaurant one time and began to talk to him about his life and what he did. I did not immediately tell him I was a preacher, so he continued to smoke his cigarette while he talked about how he didn't go to church and was living with his girlfriend. Finally he asked me what I did, so I told him I was a preacher. Then he proceeded to tell me how God spoke to him at one time to be an evangelist. I guess he thought this would impress me, but instead he was shocked when I asked him, "What are you doing about it?" This man knew what he thought was the will of God for his life, but it was of no value to him because he had made no commitment to it.

THE EXAMPLE OF THE THREE HEBREW MEN

> *Shadrach, Meshach, and Abed-Nego answered and said to the king, "O Nebuchadnezzar, we have no need to answer you in this matter. If that is the case, our God whom we serve is able to deliver us from the burning fiery furnace, and He will deliver us from your hand, O king. But if not, let it be known to you, O king, that we do not serve your gods, nor will we worship the gold image which you have set up"* (Daniel 3:16-18 NKJV).

The three Hebrew men who refuse to bow to the image of Nebuchadnezzar were committed to doing the will of God, whether that meant being delivered or being burned in the fire. Notice they said "*nor will we worship the gold image*" to the king. They exercised their will not to worship the golden image. These men knew enough of the Mosaic Law (which is a part of the Word of God) that they made a consecration and commitment that no matter what happened they would always serve God.

THE EXAMPLE OF JESUS

Jesus recognized the Old Testament Scriptures as the will of God for Him. A study of Jewish history reveals that Jewish boys were required to spend many hours learning the Scriptures. As a boy growing up, Jesus probably spent many hours studying the Old Testament Scriptures. Years later, when He was tempted in the wilderness by the devil, He knew the Scriptures well enough that He responded to every temptation, *"It is written"* (Matthew 4:4,7,10 NKJV). Throughout His life and earthly ministry, Jesus always referred to Scripture as the basis for His conduct, His direction, His defense, and His destiny.

On numerous occasions, Jesus withdrew Himself from other people to a place where He could pray alone (see Matthew 26:36; Mark 6:46; 14:32; Luke 6:12; 9:28). Part of the reason Jesus did this was to seek the instruction and will of the Father in prayer. During these times of prayer, Jesus both received knowledge of the specific issues concerning the will of God and then consecrated Himself to the will of God.

Jesus also committed Himself to the will of the Father. In John 4:34 (NKJV), He said, *"My food is to do the will of Him who sent Me, and to finish His work."* The value of Jesus knowing the will of God and coming to the earth was determined by His consecration and commitment to do the will of God. He did this by committing to what His Father said to do. In the end, His consecration and commitment enabled Him to receive the help He needed from the Father and finish His redemptive work for humankind on the Cross.

> *For I have not spoken on My own authority; but the Father*
> *who sent Me gave Me a command, what I should say and*

what I should speak. And I know that His command is everlasting life. Therefore, whatever I speak, just as the Father has told Me, so I speak (John 12:49-50 NKJV).

Then Jesus said to them, "When you lift up the Son of Man, then you will know that I am He, and that I do nothing of Myself; but as My Father taught Me, I speak these things" (John 8:28 NKJV).

The life of Jesus indicates that if a person will commit themselves to daily take in the Word of God, it will enable them to do what the Word of God tells them to do. It is impossible for anyone to fully conform to God's will without first making a commitment to intake daily from the Word of God. This shows how beneficial it is for us to make a commitment to daily read and meditate upon the Word of God.

CONTINUAL ALIGNMENT IS NECESSARY

Think about this—Jesus lived thirty-three years upon the earth, and during that time He grew and developed to where He could commit Himself to finish the work of redemption by enduring the Cross, death, and the grave. It took thirty-three years of growth and development so Jesus could fully commit to the prayer He prayed in the Garden of Gethsemane, *"Father, if it is Your will, take this cup away from Me; nevertheless not My will, but Yours, be done"* (Luke 22:42 NKJV).

Jesus proved it is possible for us to consecrate and commit our life to God's Word until we are able to do what God wants us to do. Like Jesus, we will also have to pray that prayer of consecration repeatedly until we reach that point of full consecration and determination to do God's will. Our human will doesn't always fully align with God's will right away. We are not always immediately convinced that we want to go the way God wants us to go. But if we will continue to devote ourselves more and more to God's Word and His plan for our lives, we can reach that moment when we are fully aligned with God's will and enter willingly into what He said to do. By following Jesus' example, it is possible for us to say as He did in John 17:4 (NKJV), *"I have glorified You on the earth. I have finished the work which You have given Me to do."*

CHAPTER 8

EMOTIONS: OUR INNER INFLUENCE

"Our human emotions want to be our masters, and often we unconsciously submit to them."

As a boy in school and then as a teenager, I was a left-handed softball pitcher. I had learned to be a control pitcher since I could not throw the ball faster than around sixty miles an hour. So I developed a variety of pitches to keep the batter guessing and practiced until nine times out of ten I could throw the ball across the plate where I wanted it to be. During that time I learned that although it certainly helped to be in great physical shape and have great athletic abilities, having positive thoughts and controlling my emotions was just as important. Later on, I found this to be true in many other areas of life as well.

Many people struggle with their emotions. The words of the apostle Paul describe many people's performance or reaction to things around them: *"For the good that I will to do, I do not do; but the evil I will not to do, that I practice"* (Romans 7:19 NKJV). It seems that Paul set out to do good, but something caused him to end up doing something else. Some think Paul was talking about his life before he was born again.

However, even after we are born again, often our fleshly desires and emotions still come against us doing the will of God. We are born again in our human spirit or heart, but we must stay alert and guard our emotions because they will respond much the same way as before until we retrain them to help us respond correctly in following God's will.

GOD MADE US WITH EMOTIONS

Negative emotions often pop up, seemingly out of nowhere, and sabotage many people's relationships, their work, their dreams, and their goals in life. Yet those who are able to conquer their emotions and use them in a positive way are often very successful in life. Our human emotions are perhaps one of the most influential yet neglected parts of the human makeup, although some organizations are waking up to the influence that emotions have in a person's life.

Business marketing and advertising often appeals to the emotions of people to get them involved in buying their products. Without the emotional connection, people are not easily persuaded or moved to get involved in something or buy a certain product.

The subject of human emotions has been rather controversial in the Body of Christ. Some theological scholars advocate that everything in our past contributes to or determines our present emotional state. Others practice more of a stoic type of lifestyle, rejecting the idea that emotions have any influence on a person's life and denying the emotions the right to function or be expressed much at all.

However, God created humankind with emotions to give them the ability to express themselves. After God created humanity, He looked at everything He had made, including humans with emotions as part of their makeup, and declared it was all *"very good"* (Genesis 1:31 NKJV). As we approach this subject with an open mind, we can see the subject of our human emotions is addressed in the Word of God and that the Creator of our human emotions has some instructions for us about them.

DEFINING THE HUMAN EMOTIONS

The word *emotions* is not found in some of the older versions of the Bible. However, in numerous places in the Bible we find our human emotions described in various ways. In the New King James Version we read, *"'Be angry, and do not sin': do not let the sun go down on your wrath"* (Ephesians 4:26 NKJV). *The Passion Translation* mentions the word *emotions* in its paraphrased version of this verse, *"But don't let the passion of your emotions lead you to sin! Don't let anger control you or be fuel for revenge, not for even a day."* Here we see anger described as a negative emotion that we must learn to control in our lives. Left unchecked, the emotion of anger can cause irretrievable harm and damage. It happens far too often that some person speaks rashly in anger and later wishes in vain they could take back what they said.

In Proverbs 14:30 (NKJV) we read, *"A sound heart is life to the body, but envy is rottenness to the bones."* *The Message* reads it this way: *"A sound mind makes for a robust body, but runaway emotions corrode the bones."* Envy is also a negative emotional response that can happen in the soul in certain situations or toward certain people. Most people probably have thoughts of envy once in a while but don't pay much attention to them.

However, some people allow emotions of envy to run their life and negatively influence them in their relationships with others. Uncontrolled envy has destroyed many marriage relationships, causing the person affected by an envious spouse to say that "It is impossible to live with them or please them."

THE INFLUENCE OF OUR EMOTIONS

The word *emotions* comes from the Latin word *emotus,* and it carries the idea of moving out. People are more easily moved on an emotional level than in almost any other area of their beings. Our human emotions include the capacity for both positive and negative feelings and affections such as love, hate, joy, desire, and fear. Emotions lie deep inside of us and we are often unconscious of them until they are displayed by our feelings and affections.

Often people connect with each other on an emotional level before they're willing to buy into a relationship or consider the information the person is giving out. Senator Bob Dole from Kansas was the Republican candidate in the 1996 US presidential race. Previously he had served courageously in the military during World War II, sustaining severe injuries from German machine gun fire as he tried to save another soldier. After a long recovery period, Senator Dole went on to become a lawyer and represented the state of Kansas in the US Senate for many years. Yet he hardly ever mentioned his past military achievements and the accomplishments of his political career during his presidential campaign. He kept it factual and logical, but

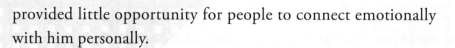

provided little opportunity for people to connect emotionally with him personally.

His opponent in the presidential race was just the opposite, appealing to the emotions of the American people with his personal charm and manners. While some say a badly run campaign was one reason for Dole's defeat on Election Day, one could argue that his lack of emotional connection with the American people was another cause for his loss.

EMOTIONS AND AFFECTIONS ARE A TARGET

We must keep in mind that most people are more susceptible in their emotions to outside motivations from other people than any other areas. Most victims of manipulation are controlled through their emotions. Proverbs 4:23 (TLB) reveals the importance of guarding our heart, or emotions, saying, *"Above all else, guard your affections. For they influence everything else in your life."*

Affections are strong emotional feelings within us that create desires for certain things or people, causing us to do something beyond what we might normally do. Sometimes we read of a person who, out of a burst of affection, may give something to one of his children or grandchildren. We have to keep in mind that most people are emotional creatures rather than creatures of logic.

FOCUS ON THE RIGHT THINGS

The Word of God instructs Christians where to set their affections, saying, *"If then you were raised with Christ, seek those things which are above, where Christ is, sitting at the right hand of God. Set your mind on things above, not on things on the earth"* (Colossians 3:1-2 NKJV). Setting our mind and affections on higher things is very important because they play a huge role in determining the path we travel in life. They affect the relationships we build, the vocation we pursue, and the things we accomplish in life. People usually go in the direction of their affections and passions. Throughout life, we'll see many things that seem good as we look at them, but only a few will impact our heart. The people or things that touch our heart are the things we often pursue to obtain or have a relationship with.

To be successful in life we must learn to focus our emotional affections in the areas we want to excel in. We can't achieve great things while being affectionate for little things that are of no consequence. A shared trait of many people in human history who did uncommon feats and accomplished much were those who learned to control and direct their affections and emotions toward what they wanted to be or do.

EXAMPLES OF HUMAN EMOTIONS

God gave over some people who insisted on pursuing perverted relationships to vile affections and lusts (see Romans 1:26; Colossians 3:5). Some people's involvement in certain corrupt or immoral things cause them to be without natural affections or the ability to cherish affectionately, and they eventually become hard-hearted (see Romans 1:31; Titus 3:3). These things cause much damage to the human emotions, so much so that they no longer function as God created them.

Believers are to crucify the flesh with its affections, emotions, and influences. Crucifixion involves something undergone with hardship and pain, indicating that a death is necessary (see Galatians 5:24). Many people draw back from dealing with their emotions and affections. However, those who live at the level of life that God planned for them have learned how to control their emotions and willfully put to death wrong emotions that would hinder them in pursuing God's will.

Paul affectionately desired and longed for the Thessalonian church (see 1 Thessalonians 2:8). Titus had an inward affection (tender mercy, sympathy, and pity) toward the Corinthian church (see 2 Corinthians 7:13-15). This indicates that in a positive way we can direct our emotions to help us attain what God wants us to do in our lives.

BIBLICAL THOUGHTS ABOUT EMOTIONS

There are numerous Scriptures from various translations that mention the subject of emotions. Look at the following verses:

> *Joseph could no longer control his emotions in front of everyone who was standing around him, so he cried out, "Have everyone leave me!" No one else was there when Joseph told his brothers who he was* (Genesis 45:1 GW).

> *Why am I so overwrought? Why am I so disturbed? Why can't I just hope in God? Despite all my emotions, I will believe and praise the One who saves me and is my life* (Psalm 42:5 VOICE).

> *O my soul, come, praise the Eternal with all that is in me—body, emotions, mind, and will—every part of who I am-praise His holy name* (Psalm 103:1 VOICE).

> *A fool expresses all his emotions, but a wise person controls them* (Proverbs 29:11 GW).

> *Then God's peace, which goes beyond anything we can imagine, will guard your thoughts and emotions through Christ Jesus* (Philippians 4:7 GW).

EXAMINING OUR EMOTIONS

The Word of God is able to penetrate and work in our soul and spirit. The writer of the book of Hebrews reveals the power of the Word of God, saying, *"For the word of God is living and powerful, and sharper than any two-edged sword, piercing even to the division of soul and spirit, and of joints and marrow, and is a discerner of the thoughts and intents of the heart"* (Hebrews 4:12 NKJV). Just as a sword is able to penetrate the physical body, the Word of God, under the direction of the Holy Spirit, is powerful and able to penetrate our soul and spirit and change us according to the will of God.

Our human emotions are located deep within us, and sometimes it is hard to distinguish between our emotions and our heart. Only by sitting under the Word of God over a period of time will we know the difference. Our emotions can be ministered to by the Word of God in controlled situations with the right atmosphere and with the help of the Holy Spirit. At times, the Holy Spirit will bring certain emotions and feelings to our conscious mind that are hindering our Christian development. As this happens, we can identify them and deal with them effectively according to the Word of God.

TAKE A "WORD BATH"

That is why we need to take "Word baths" according to Ephesians 5:26 on a regular and continual basis. Reading the Word of God, believing it, and speaking the Word to ourselves will create an atmosphere that allows the Holy Spirit to reveal our emotions and desires to us.

When a silversmith wants to refine silver to a certain level of purity, he first heats the silver ore until it is in a liquid form and then carefully removes the dross that comes to the surface. This process may have to be done several times until the refining process results in silver at the level of desired purity. Just as silver is purified through the refining process, our soul can also be purified through the fire of the Holy Spirit as He applies the Word of God.

The "impurities" of the soul—such as hurts, wounds, and bruises—can be removed from our emotional arena by the work of the Holy Spirit when they come to the surface of our conscious mind. We may read or hear something, a person may say something, or something may happen that triggers an emotional response from us. At that point, those emotions that were lying deep within us rise to our conscious thought life, and while they are there on the surface of our consciousness, the Holy Spirit will help us in receiving the healing we need.

HELP FOR OUR EMOTIONS

The most expensive thing we can do is to hold a grudge or unforgiveness against another person. The effect upon our soul is harmful when we do these things. If we want our entire life to be healthy and functioning well, we need to keep the emotional part of our being clean by reading the Word and allowing the Holy Spirit to minister to us during our personal devotion time.

We must believe that God wants to help us deal with our emotions and that He can help us. There are three biblical actions we can take to facilitate the removal of soulish impurities and receive God's help to have a healthy soul: 1) acknowledge the problem or need; 2) affirm God's ability to help us; and 3) ask for God's help. These actions are necessary in dealing with our emotions, and they can be implemented whenever these emotional feelings rise to our conscious mind. These actions are also how we receive salvation and other things from God.

#1: Acknowledge the Problem or Need

We begin by acknowledging the existence of the emotional hurts, wounds, and bruises in our soul. We must also acknowledge or admit the truth to ourselves that we are unable to deal with these things on our own. Finally, we turn to God to acknowledge that we are unable to deal with those hurts, wounds, and bruises by our own efforts and that we need His help.

#2: Affirm God's Ability

Next, we must verbally declare that God is able to take care of our hurts, wounds, and bruises by quoting Scriptures that relate to our situation. This helps us to believe God will help us in every area of life, including our emotions. God is able to do what He has promised and is willing to do it for everyone who comes to Him. Satan may tempt us to hide our hurts, but instead we must quickly run to God for help.

#3: Ask God to Help Us

We should not be afraid to ask God to deal with these things as only He can. He has promised to forgive us and enable us to forgive by the power of the Holy Spirit. God is the One who promised to be our Helper (see Hebrews 13:5) and to *perfect that which concerns me*" (Psalm 138:8 NKJV). Yet He works with us according to our faith. Exercising our faith gives God permission to help us in our lives and allows God to bring healing to our soul. So we must believe His Word and ask Him to do what He has promised.

DEALING WITH EMOTIONS IS A PROCESS

Sometimes applying biblical instructions to our lives seems painful to us. The old things of the past have been a part of our lives for so long and now they need to be changed or removed. Galatians 5:24 tells us to crucify the affections and emotions of the flesh, revealing that a death to our fleshly emotions and desires is necessary so we can embrace the new attitudes and move up to the level of life God intended.

We wish this would all happen instantaneously. However, soulish things don't normally work that way; it is a process over a period of time. In 1 Corinthians 15:31 (NKJV) Paul said, *"I die daily."* This is not a pleasant thought. We naturally shrink from anything that has to do with death. Also, Paul stated, *"if by the Spirit you put to death the deeds of the body, you will live"* (Romans 8:13 NKJV). The Good News is that, with the help of the Holy Spirit, we can submit to dying daily to our personal desires, hurts, ambitions, griefs, etc. so we can be used effectively by God in ministering to others.

Some years ago, I was trained by a hospital chaplain to help people who find out they or someone they love has no hope for recovery and that death is inevitable. He told me there are five emotional aspects that usually happen during the process of losing a loved one. These five aspects include: 1) denial, 2) anger, 3) bargaining, 4) depression, and 5) acceptance—people accepting what happened and that they can live a normal life again in spite of what happened.

These emotional aspects do not always happen in the same order; often one or more of these aspects shows up repeatedly or in a seemingly random way. But we'll find that these aspects of emotional grief are often triggered by something that someone said, something that reminded us of our loss, or we find ourselves in a similar situation.

SANCTIFY THE EMOTIONS WITH THE WORD

These emotional aspects related to grief can happen in various degrees not only when loved ones pass away, but also when we suffer abuse or loss of any kind. This may help us understand the process we're going through emotionally and give us hope that wholeness and a normal life is possible again for us. These aspects can explain why we're acting in a certain way, such as experiencing times of anger even though we are not normally an angry person. Understanding this can also assure us that we are normal people even though life doesn't seem very normal at the moment.

It's important to deal with these things correctly and not let these emotions of grief, hurt, or loss take root and become a permanent part of our lives. Unfortunately, some people get stuck in the middle of these emotional issues. Others refuse to acknowledge their emotional needs and become bitter or hardened, and in some cases they end up with a warped or skewed view of life and what to expect from God.

No matter where we are in the process of dealing with our emotions, the Word of God can help us as we believe it and speak it to ourselves. Christ wants to sanctify and cleanse us *"with the washing of water by the word"* (Ephesians 5:26 NKJV). Our body needs cleansing periodically to be free from the dirt and grime of our work. Likewise, our emotions also need cleansing from time to time when hurts, wounds, and losses happen to us. As we daily affirm to ourselves that God is working, helping, cleansing, and perfecting us, He will bring wholeness to our emotions and make it possible for us to step up to new levels of life.

ONE MAN'S STORY OF VICTORY

Several years ago, I met a man named Jon (not his real name) who had experienced severe emotional damage as a child. Jon grew up in a very authoritarian home and church setting. He was abused verbally, physically, nutritionally, and emotionally. He tried hard to please his father but found it impossible. His parents' marriage was constantly in strife and ended when his father died of cancer. Fear of what Jon had seen in his parents' marriage kept him from getting married.

He tried to get free of the authoritarian church he grew up in, but he couldn't seem to break its legalistic hold. In his search for help, as a young man he turned to drugs and occult activity. Finally when Jon was forty years old, he became born again and left the church he had grown up in. He began attending another church, but sadly he experienced verbal and emotional abuse from those church leaders as well.

Finally, in a time of emotional turmoil, Jon reached out to a minister for help. The minister met with him weekly for several years to teach, encourage, confront, and support his every step. This time of being taught the Word of God allowed the Holy Spirit to wash and cleanse his mind and emotions until he was able to rise up and step into a new life. From that time on he renewed his mind daily with God's Word and regained control of his emotions so he could follow God's will for His life. Today he is a healthy, normal individual who actively serves in his church and is a blessing to others.

Jon's victory over what happened to him did not happen instantaneously. It was a process of God changing Jon's soul and getting his emotions healthy again over a period of time. Some days it seemed he made great strides in renewing his mind and ministering to his emotions, and other days it seemed as if no progress was made at all. Yet Jon did not give up, and eventually he was able to successfully live a new life in Christ. His story of recovering from severe emotional hurts and wounds gives us hope for overcoming our emotional problems as well.

CHAPTER 9

GETTING A GRIP ON OUR EMOTIONS

*"Don't allow yourself to be sabotaged
by your emotions; instead, learn
to use them for your benefit."*

The first time I was invited to preach, it was at a little storefront church with about fifty people. I was just a young guy, and I was excited about the opportunity. But I also knew about two men in that church who gave a (usually negative and critical) review of the preacher and their message. As I began to preach, I got emotional, choked up, and finally got through the message the best I could. Most of the people were very kind and supportive as I tried to preach. Sure enough, after the service those two guys came to me with a very negative review about my preaching. I went home devastated, not only because of what they had said but also because my emotions had gotten out of control. I determined to somehow get a grip on my emotions before I was asked to preach again.

Many people have damaged emotions because of what they have experienced in life. Trauma and tragedy can scar a person emotionally until they don't function well in relationships or respond well to life situations. A person may have recovered physically from something that happened, but they can still be emotionally challenged by it. For many, the emotional scars within affect them more than the physical scars they bear on the outside. The truth is, winning in life has a lot to do with having healthy emotions.

MANY HAVE DAMAGED EMOTIONS

Many people live with damaged emotions that affect what they do in life. I visited with one lady who made daily visits to the grave site of her husband who had passed away over fifteen years before. She told me she would cry every day as she sat there by his grave.

One man I talked with was in a battle in which all of the other soldiers in his platoon had died. Many years later, this man still suffered emotionally from the horrors of that battle and from feeling guilty because of being the only survivor.

Another older man told me he had never gotten married because of the awful abuse and conflict he saw in his parents' marriage. He said he had tried to get married several times, but each time he got engaged he felt as if he was suffocating emotionally and called it off. Emotionally these people had not recovered from what they had experienced in their past.

THE VALUE OF GOD'S WORD

We must look to God's Word for the healing and support we need for our emotions. The Creator of our emotions provided a way to fix them when they are damaged. Look at Isaiah 53:5 (NKJV) for a moment: *"But He was wounded for our transgressions, He was bruised for our iniquities; the chastisement for our peace was upon Him, and by His stripes we are healed."*

This verse speaks prophetically of the substitutional suffering of Christ at Calvary's Cross for humankind. It indicates that healing was provided in the plan of redemption for the whole person— spirit, soul, and body. *"But He was wounded for our transgressions, He was bruised for our iniquities"* applies to our spirit; *"the chastisement for our peace was upon Him"* applies to our soul; and *"by His stripes we are healed"* applies to our physical body. When we know that God has provided healing for the whole person in His plan of redemption, we can come to God with confidence to receive the healing we need.

God wants us to realize the importance of trusting His Word to help our emotions. We can apply our faith in God's Word to our emotions just like any other area in which we have a need. As we begin to believe and speak the Word of God, it creates an arena wherein God can bring healing, our soul can act in a healthy way, and it sets boundaries for the actions of our soul.

So speaking God's Word consistently over our emotions will eventually help us to respond in better and healthier ways to the different situations we face in life. Believing and speaking God's Word strengthens us to deal with the weaknesses and flaws in our soul and helps us resist the impulses and emotional cravings that are not in line with the Word of God.

OVERCOMING HARMFUL EMOTIONS

Many people deal with low self-esteem and rejection, which often shows up in their emotional behavior. Reading and studying Ephesians 1:3-13 is a great place to find out how God looks at us, what He had done for us at Calvary, and who we are in Christ as believers.

For example, in Ephesians 1:6 we see that God has already accepted us through Christ's redemptive work at the Cross. This means we don't have to let other people's acceptance or rejection of us determine our value and self-worth. Consequently, when we raise our self-esteem by renewing our mind to God's Word, we can expect to have better and healthier emotional responses in whatever situation we're in.

The Word of God is the one thing that will consistently minister to our emotions. Nothing else can bring real change to our lives like the Word of God can. Reading the Word can be a healing balm to our soul just like water is to a parched body. There may be other spiritual things and even things in the natural that we can do to help our emotions. However, we should always apply the Word of God along with whatever else we do to help improve our emotional condition.

We can apply the Word of God by speaking His promises over our emotions. Our emotions are created to respond to our voice. If we speak the healing promises repeatedly to our emotions, eventually a healing process will take place.

SPEAKING TO OUR EMOTIONS

Satan will try to attack us in the area of our emotions because he knows that is often where people are weak and don't know what to do. So we have to stand in our spiritual authority and speak directly to our emotions, declaring, *"Satan, leave my emotions alone in Jesus' name! Emotions, be whole in Jesus' name. I declare that I am in control of my emotions. Emotions, you will help me in living my life and not hinder me. Thank You, Father, that You have made me free in Jesus' name."*

Early in my Christian life, I began to apply the Word of God to my emotions by standing in front of the mirror in our bathroom, looking at my reflection in the mirror, and saying, *"Satan, I bind you and declare that you cannot use my emotions against me! Emotions, you listen to me. From now on you will serve me and not sabotage my life. You will help me and not hinder me. You will do what I say, in Jesus' name."* I continued to speak this way to my emotions several times a day until I no longer had any unwanted emotional displays, and this allowed God to use me in a much greater way.

OTHER WAYS TO HELP OUR EMOTIONS

There are a number of other ways to minister to our emotions. Music, especially praise and worship music, will minister to our emotions. Matthew 8:2-3 (NKJV) gives the account when *"a leper came and worshiped Him, saying, 'Lord, if You are willing, You can make me clean.' Then Jesus put out His hand and touched him, saying, 'I am willing; be cleansed.' Immediately his leprosy was cleansed."* As we worship God, His healing power will manifest, not just for our physical body but also for our soul.

Periodically, King Saul was troubled by an evil spirit, tormented with depression and fear, and could not sleep. He kept David at his palace to play the harp whenever the evil spirit troubled him. *"David would play the harp and Saul would feel better, and the evil spirit would go away"* (1 Samuel 16:23 TLB). Saul's mental and emotional condition was soothed and found relief from listening to David's music.

Getting into an atmosphere where the presence of God is tangible is another way to minister to our emotions. Psalm 16:11 (NKJV) tells us that, *"You will show me the path of life; in Your presence is fullness of joy; at Your right hand are pleasures forevermore."* Wonderful benefits are found in an atmosphere that is saturated with the presence of God. This is where the life and health of God can flow freely through our whole being, touching and ministering to every part of our being as needed. There are various ways we can create an atmosphere where the presence of God is manifested. Sometimes we do this by reading and proclaiming the promises of God's Word; sometimes it's through worshiping and praising God. At other times God's presence is experienced as we pour out our heart out to God in prayer, or at times with tears of repentance and weeping (see Psalm 30:5; 126:5).

THE HEALING EFFECT OF NATURE

Spending time in a nature setting is another way we can find therapeutic healing for our emotions. It is significant that when God created man, He put him in a garden instead of a building. God created human beings and originally placed them in a garden, not in a building. This nature setting was a natural habitat for them where they were surrounded by the beauty and tranquility of God's handiwork.

However, if humankind is moved out of their natural habitat into something less, it has a downward effect on our soul. A constant environment of constant concrete, asphalt, loud noises, sirens, cars honking, gunfire, and explosions will cause our mind to lose its sense of peace and creativity. At that point, it is difficult to hear God's voice speaking to us. That's why people slip so easily into doubt, fear, and unbelief instead of believing God will help them.

God created us to be believers. Occasionally everyone has thoughts of doubt, but this is not the normal thought pattern for a believer. Believing in God and His Word is normal for every Christian. The first several verses in Psalm 23:1-3 reveal the impact that spending time in a nature setting can have in restoring our soul until it returns to a healthy condition of believing and trusting in God's promises.

> *The Lord is my shepherd; I shall not want* (Psalm 23:1 NKJV).

When you observe the grandeur and awesomeness of nature, it will help you realize how big God really is. Matthew 6:30 (KJV) tells us, *"Wherefore, if God so clothe the grass of the field, which to day is, and to morrow is cast into the oven, shall he not much more clothe you, O ye of little faith?"* If God can take care of the things in nature and make all things work together, how much more does He take care of us and make everything work together for our good?

Nature provides a picture of a big God who is able and powerful enough to meet our every need. He can do things far beyond our human ability to accomplish. Being surrounded by the majesty and beauty of nature helps us to realize that God has literally provided everything we need for our existence.

He makes me to lie down in green pastures; He leads me beside the still waters (Psalm 23:2 NKJV).

Notice that God leads us to lie down in green pastures. God brings us into a place of rest, peace, beauty, and abundance—not into barren and desolate places. Rest and peace are essential to our well-being. Being in a peaceful environment surrounded by the tranquility of nature can have a tremendous healing effect upon our emotions.

I have talked with people who are constantly busy, both mentally and physically. They said they can't sleep at night because their mind and emotions are still racing with thousands of thoughts. One lady told me, "If my mind was a race horse, I'd cross the finish line in first place!" But periodic rest for both our soul and body is essential for the well-being of our soul. God designed us to function in a rhythm of work and rest, of performance and recuperation, and of being busy and holding still.

He restores my soul; He leads me in the paths of righteousness for His name's sake (Psalm 23:3 NKJV).

The word *restores* means to return to or to go back to something or to bring something back. The idea is to repeatedly return to the same place or condition we have previously been. We often have to take time from our busy schedules to return to having a peaceful mindset and healthy emotions.

Restoration in our soul can be maximized as we are surrounded by God's handiwork displayed in nature. Everywhere we look we can see God, for nature represents its Creator. In that setting of nature's beauty, healing and restoration can happen in our soul, affecting every part of our mind, will, and emotions.

MY STORY OF HEALING

I remember a time when I went through a period of great difficulty in my life and ministry. Things had not worked out as we had hoped in the church we had been pastoring, and we were devastated. And because of what had happened at that church, we no longer believed we could successfully pastor a church. We told people we didn't have what it took to be a pastor.

We ended up living in rural Florida, renting a small house trailer a half mile off the main highway, surrounded by a huge swamp and giant pine trees. The first thing I noticed was the quietness and solitude there. There were no sounds of sirens, traffic, or people talking. Occasionally, we did hear an airplane fly overhead. Often the loudest thing we heard was the wind gently moving through the pine trees. It seemed as if we were in a world of our own, locked away from the hustle and bustle of the outside world. It took several days for me to adjust to the serenity and solitude of nature around me and begin to relax.

During that time, God took me to a Scripture in Psalm 46:10 (NKJV), *"Be still, and know that I am God."* Most people are afraid to get quiet because of what they might find out about themselves. But in the quietness and solitude of nature, I found God revealing Himself to me and ministering to me over and over again. And it was there in that setting that God restored my soul and I started believing again that I could do what God had called me to do.

Yes, God spoke to me in my heart, but He also ministered to me through the nature setting I was in. Often the quietness of my surroundings would saturate my soul and the presence of God's peace would engulf me until my soul was in a state of joy, peace, and serenity. I began to speak the promises of God to myself and my emotions on a daily basis, restoring hope and health to my soul. We stayed there for almost a year until my emotions were healthy and the hope of my calling was once again restored to me.

MINISTERING TO OUR EMOTIONS

Other things that will minister to our emotions include humor and laughter (see Proverbs 17:22), hobbies or recreation of some kind, and physical exercise. Physical exercise can help stimulate the blood circulation and provide fresh oxygen to our brain and help our soul to function better.

Different things work for different people. We should look for things that will minister to our soul and emotions, such as 1) things that cause a break in our daily routine, 2) things that produce peace of mind, and 3) things that make us feel good about ourselves.

We can always receive help for our emotions from the Word of God. That should be the first thing we turn to when we need emotional help. Nothing can take the place of God's Word in ministering to our soul. Reading, believing, and speaking the Word of God can have a great healing effect upon our emotions.

CAUSES OF EMOTIONAL PROBLEMS

The apostle Peter instructs us to *"abstain from fleshly lusts which war against the soul"* (1 Peter 2:11 NKJV). He warns that just going after fleshly or material things instead of pursuing the righteous things of God can have a negative effect upon the soul. If our priorities and actions aren't in line with the Word of God, our mind and emotions

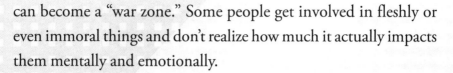

can become a "war zone." Some people get involved in fleshly or even immoral things and don't realize how much it actually impacts them mentally and emotionally.

When we yield to fleshly lusts, it opens the door for a deluge of carnal and sinful thoughts accompanied by emotions of shame, guilt, and condemnation to flood our mind and impact our emotions. The idea presented in this verse is as if someone brings a military campaign against our soul. So we need to guard against these fleshly lusts that satan fires like arrows against our soul. We must take offensive action by making the Word of God a high priority in our lives. This will stabilize us and help us stay emotionally healthy.

THE NEED TO FORGIVE

Two prominent causes for having emotional problems are 1) failure to receive forgiveness, and 2) failure to give forgiveness. The Scriptures place a high importance on forgiveness (see Matthew 18:21-22; Mark 11:25; Ephesians 4:32). If we harbor unforgiveness in our heart, it can lead to having problems in our soul, entertaining wrong thoughts, and emotionally responding to life's problems the wrong way.

I have known people who refuse to forgive those who didn't treat them right, and I watched them go through mental and emotional difficulties. Emotions of anger, resentment, bitterness, fear, and being critical showed up in their lives. They had to contend with thoughts and emotions of anger, guilt, condemnation, and a sense of unworthiness. I have also seen some people become very controlling and manipulative in relationships to make sure the hurtful things of the past won't happen to them again.

As this process continued, these people seemed to lose their ability to distinguish between actual facts and their perception of things. The Word of God was no longer the absolute governing factor in their lives. They used only the portion of the Word of God that justified their position or that they thought applied to the other person. Some of those people contracted physical diseases such as cancer or arthritis. Many physical diseases have inroads into people's lives because of their spiritual and soulish conditions.

Some people readily forgive others but won't forgive themselves. They are harder on themselves than God is. But Matthew 22:39 (NKJV) reveals that we are to love others as we do ourselves: *"You shall love your neighbor as yourself."* The devil brings up things from our past to torment us, even if we have already applied the blood of Jesus Christ and asked God to forgive us of those things.

But we must learn to believe the Word of God no matter what the devil tells us. Romans 3:4 (NKJV) declares, *"Let God be true but every man a liar."* This means we must choose to believe what the Word of God tells us about ourselves rather than what we're feeling or experiencing. We must give careful consideration to God's Word instead of listening to others' opinions or what the devil is telling us.

EVIDENCE OF DAMAGED EMOTIONS

Sometimes people need help in realizing what is not healthy in their life. Some people have been in bad situations their whole life and they don't even realize it's unhealthy. They may have been in this condition so long that they think it's normal and may act surprised or even get upset when someone mentions their situation is not good. So a person may not be aware of their need for help or that God wants to help them get to a place of being healthy and whole.

Evidence of having damaged emotions may include things like having a severe or continual sense of unworthiness, feeling like nothing is ever good or perfect enough, being overly sensitive to what others say or do to you, or being constantly fearful. Some psychologists also include perverted sex as both a cause and evidence of damaged emotions.

Sometimes it is helpful to ask ourselves questions like the following to help determine if emotional problems exist that need to be dealt with:

▶ "Do I hold strong resentment or bitterness toward those who did this to me?"

▶ "Does resentment still rise up in me when I hear their names or meet them?"

▶ "Have I allowed the blood of Christ to cleanse me of all unforgiveness, or am I still holding unforgiveness toward others for what they did or toward myself for letting this happen?"

▶ "Do I really love those who did this and want God's best for them?"

▶ "Am I being truthful in attaching blame or responsibility for the situation, or am I unfairly blaming others and justifying myself?"

▶ "Have I accepted responsibility for what has happened, and for my present condition, or am I making excuses for it?"

Our emotional condition will change if we continue to believe and speak the Word of God. First John 1:9 (NKJV) assures us that, *"If we confess our sins, He is faithful and just to forgive us our sins and to cleanse us from all unrighteousness."* We must choose to believe what 1 John 1:9 tells us rather than letting the devil torment us with his accusations and lies.

YOU CAN HAVE VICTORY

There are other causes for emotional problems—such as demonic influence, perverted sex, and abusive relationships—but many of the answers to these problems are found in the Word of God. Sometimes along with believing and speaking God's Word, people also need the help of a professional counselor to guide them step by step in the journey to overcome these deep-rooted problems.

Not getting professional help when it is needed can lead to bigger problems in a person's life. There is no shame in getting help from a competent professional when a person needs it. Proverbs 1:5 (NKJV) tells us, *"A wise man will hear and increase learning, and a man of understanding will attain wise counsel."* Also Proverbs 24:6 (NKJV) states that, *"For by wise counsel you will wage your own war, and in a multitude of counselors there is safety."*

We can have victory in the area of our emotions, but we must understand the rules that apply to having a healthy soul. To be successful in this area, we must remember to spend time reading and meditating on God's Word. This will help us emotionally as well as spiritually. Allowing God to lead us into places that are peaceful and restful and choosing to spend time there will help our emotions be ministered to and receive the healing they need. Finally, it is important to speak the Word of God to our emotions, even in the midst of difficulties, because this will help us get a grip on our emotions.

PART THREE

DEVELOPING OUR SOUL
FOR THE NEXT LEVEL

I have come to give you everything in
abundance, more than you expect—
life in its fullness until you overflow!
—Jesus Christ, John 10:10 TPT

CHAPTER 10

KNOWING JESUS AS OUR HEALER

"Jesus knows what we have been through, and He can heal every hurt, remove every sorrow, and help us in every situation."

Several years ago my youngest brother was diagnosed with a very rare kind of cancer that the doctors said only comes by being exposed to certain things like asbestos. I asked God for healing for my brother, fervently believing in God's healing promises. But despite my best efforts to pray effectively for him, my brother passed away. I became angry at the unfairness of the situation and others who thought it was God's will for him to die at a young age. Emotionally, I was hurting as I grieved over losing a brother. It was only as I turned to God's Word that I discovered Someone who knew how I felt and could actually bring healing to me.

It seems that sooner or later we all go through difficult times in life in which we experience trouble, suffer unfair treatment, deal with rejection, face criticism, and are caught in the pangs of sorrow at the passing of a loved one. Even people we would consider spiritual are not exempt from the crises of life.

GOD IS OUR HELP IN TIME OF TROUBLE

The psalmist cried out in the midst of great difficulty, *"For my soul is full of troubles, and my life draws near to the grave"* (Psalm 88:3 NKJV). In the rest of the chapter, he goes on to describe some of the troublesome thoughts in his mind. Yet he recognizes God alone is his salvation—that God alone is able to pull him out of the pit of despair and keep him from continuing the downward descent to the grave.

In times of trouble, we often feel as if no one really knows the hurt and pain we're dealing with. It doesn't seem possible that others could understand the gamut of emotions and hurt that we really feel. People say kind things, show support, drop in to check on us, and do what they can. This helps us for a moment, but these things alone cannot bring real healing for our hurts on the inside.

I have seen people who have allowed the trouble or tragedy they went through to change what they believe about God. Some even blame God for all of their troubles and the tragedies they have encountered. They once believed God would do as He promised, but now because God did not do what they thought He should do the way they thought He should, they have drawn away from Him. They no longer believe God cares about them. Instead of coming to God for help and healing, they moved further away from the one Person who could really help them.

GOD CONSTANTLY CARES FOR US

However, God doesn't change who He is whenever we go through something. God's nature does not change; He is still a good God just as the Scriptures tell us. God's Word remains unchanged; He has promised to help and heal us no matter what has happened to us. God's love toward us is unchanging; He still loves us as He did before tragedy struck. These truths about God never change.

It may be true that we don't feel like God cares, but He does. It may seem that God is far away and doesn't care what has happened to us or how we feel. The truth is, over 2,000 years ago God foresaw what we would be going through and cared enough to make provision for us through Jesus Christ at the Cross.

JESUS UNDERSTANDS WHAT WE GO THROUGH

Jesus Christ is the one Person who can always understand what we feel when others mistreat us, the despair and sorrow we feel when tragedies occur, and the hopelessness that seeks to invade our soul about things we cannot change. In all of these things, He is able to bring healing to us. No one has suffered to the depth that He did in His sufferings during His crucifixion for the sins of all humankind. Being both the Son of God and also the Son of Man enabled Him to fully identify with our sufferings, hurts, and wounds and still bring healing to us.

> *Seeing then that we have a great High Priest who has passed through the heavens, Jesus the Son of God, let us hold fast our confession. For we do not have a High Priest who cannot sympathize with our weaknesses, but was in all points tempted as we are, yet without sin. Let*

us therefore come boldly to the throne of grace, that we may obtain mercy and find grace to help in time of need (Hebrews 4:14-16 NKJV).

The Word of God states that Jesus understands our human weaknesses by virtue of becoming a man who walked upon this earth like us and suffered beyond what any other human being has ever suffered. By looking at the life of Christ and studying what Paul wrote in his epistles, we can understand where to get help for our weaknesses and frailties.

JESUS KNOWS HOW WE FEEL

Jesus is not only touched with the facts of our infirmities (the crippling, the weakness, the emotional hang-ups, and the inner conflicts) but also the feelings of our infirmities (the frustrations, anxiety, depression, hurts, rejection, loneliness). This word "feeling" comes from the Greek word *sumpatheo,* which portrays a person who is affected with the same feeling as someone else or to sympathize with someone. Elsewhere in Scripture, this word gives the idea of being touched with the feeling of another's situation or to have fellow feelings with another because they identify with what someone is going through and how they feel. This helps us to see that Jesus was affected with the same feelings as we are, and He has compassion for us.

The word *infirmities* used in Hebrews 4:15 refers to feebleness in either body or mind. In some cases, this word includes the idea of having a disease, weakness, or sickness. Infirmities or weaknesses are not necessarily sins, but they can undermine our resistance to temptation. They can cause us to be inclined to sin, sometimes without a conscious choice on our part. This may especially apply to areas in which our resistance is weak. That is one reason why Hebrews 12:1 (NKJV) admonishes us to *"lay aside every weight, and the sin which so easily ensnares us, and let us run with endurance the race that is set before us."*

JESUS IS MOVED WITH COMPASSION

Numerous times in the Gospels we read that Jesus was moved with compassion for people and healed them. Referring to Jesus, Matthew 12:20 (NKJV) says, *"A bruised reed He will not break, and smoking flax He will not quench."* He straightened and strengthened people who were like bruised reeds instead of breaking them off and discarding them. Jesus breathed life and healing upon those whose life was like smoking flax until they were burning brightly again. This shows clearly that Jesus cares about us as we go through this life.

Sometimes we feel condemned or ashamed because of what has happened to us in life. Yet this verse tells us to come to the throne of grace—the place that we in ourselves don't deserve to come to, nor are we qualified to receive anything there. Yet because of Jesus, it is at the throne of grace that we can receive hope, help, and healing for our lives. He knows all about how we feel and what we need. He is our deliverer from evil, the mender of our broken lives, and the healer of our every hurt, whether it be physical, emotional, or spiritual.

JESUS CAN IDENTIFY WITH US

Who, in the days of His flesh, when He had offered up prayers and supplications, with vehement cries and tears to Him who was able to save Him from death, and was heard because of His godly fear, though He was a Son, yet He learned obedience by the things which He suffered (Hebrews 5:7-8 NKJV).

Nothing we can experience here on earth is outside the parameters of what Jesus experienced while He was upon this earth. We cannot suffer worse than He did. In Matthew 26:38 (NKJV) Jesus said, *"My soul is exceedingly sorrowful, even to death."* This describes Jesus experiencing unimaginable torment and agony in His soul in the Garden of Gethsemane as He yielded His will to the idea of suffering death as a mortal man.

Jesus was indeed the Son of Man, but He was also the sinless Son of God and had never tasted death before. He had to yield His will to experience death for the sake of sinful humanity. He who said He is life had to undergo death for the sake of all humankind (see John 14:6).

During His earthly ministry, Jesus suffered the sharp pangs of betrayal and being forsaken by His disciples. When Judas Iscariot betrayed Jesus and led the men to the Garden of Gethsemane to arrest Him, He said, *"Judas, are you betraying the Son of Man with a kiss?"* (Luke 22:48 NKJV). Jesus was forsaken by all. He said to Peter, *"'What! Could you not watch with Me one hour?' ...Then all the disciples forsook Him and fled"* (Matthew 26:40,56 NKJV). In His most difficult hour, Jesus experienced being left all alone with no one in this earth to whom He could turn for help.

JESUS KNOWS THE FEELING OF OUR PAIN

Jesus felt the deep pain of people rejecting Him as the Messiah and being the contemptible object of scorn and disdain at His trial and crucifixion. The prophet Isaiah spoke prophetically of Him, saying, *"He is despised and rejected by men, a Man of sorrows and acquainted with grief. And we hid, as it were, our faces from Him; He was despised, and we did not esteem Him"* (Isaiah 53:3 NKJV).

Jesus also endured false accusations and mockery at His trial. He was made the object of hatred and ridicule by Jews and Romans alike. *"Then they spat in His face and beat Him; and others struck Him with the palms of their hands"* (Matthew 26:67 NKJV). Then He was mocked and forsaken on the Cross. *"If You are the Son of God, come down from the cross"* (Matthew 27:40 NKJV). The Scriptures tell us that while hanging on the cross, Jesus cried with a loud voice, *"My God, My God, why have You forsaken Me?"* (Matthew 27:46 NKJV). Jesus personally knows the feelings and emotions we experience because of things that happened in our past or because of what is happening to us at the present time. He is able to help us with every need we have.

Not only did Jesus suffer during His physical life, but He also was made sin for us at the Cross (see 2 Corinthians 5:21). Spiritually, the sin of the world was laid upon Jesus. The Cross is a major point of God identifying with humankind. Because of this, Jesus knows how sin feels, along with the guilt, condemnation, shame, and the unworthiness that comes with it.

COME TO THE THRONE OF GRACE

Let us also lay aside every encumbrance and the sin which so easily entangles us, and let us run with endurance the race that is set before us, fixing our eyes on Jesus, the author and perfecter of faith, who for the joy set before Him endured the cross, despising the shame, and has set down at the right hand of the throne of God. For consider Him who has endured such hostility by sinners against Himself, so that you will not grow weary and lose heart (Hebrews 12:1-3 NASB1995).

The throne of grace exists because of all that Jesus went through in His trial, crucifixion, death, burial, and resurrection for us. The Innocent One endured the pain of the Cross for the guilty. And it is at the throne of grace that our repentant heart encounters God's redemptive provision and the blood of Jesus Christ can be applied to the doorposts of our heart and cleanse us from all unrighteousness. There the unbearable weight of sin is removed from our soul, and we become free from the torturous thoughts and harassments of the enemy.

We as Christians are born again, but we are not perfect. When we yield to the temptation of sin, the Holy Spirit will convict us to come quickly to the throne of grace where undeserved mercy and grace is freely extended to us. God does not want us to sin, nor does He overlook sin in our lives. But when we come to the throne of grace with a repentant heart, even repeatedly, then the blood of Christ wipes out every charge listed against us and washes away every trace of sin, guilt, shame, and condemnation.

We must remember that whatever we're experiencing is not unfamiliar to Jesus. He has suffered far beyond the depth any other human being has suffered or ever will suffer. In addition to Jesus identifying with humankind at Calvary through what He suffered, He also made it possible for man to identify with Him in His resurrection from the dead and in His victory over satan, sin, and every other evil power.

Christ's redemptive work has indeed provided for the whole man, spirit, soul, and body. He is able to save us to the uttermost, freely granting forgiveness and healing to us, no matter how deep or traumatic our sin, our wounds, or our hurts may be.

JESUS' VICTORY IS OUR VICTORY

> *But thanks be to God, who gives us the victory through our Lord Jesus Christ* (1 Corinthians 15:57 NKJV).

> *Now thanks be to God who always leads us in triumph in Christ, and through us diffuses the fragrance of His knowledge in every place* (2 Corinthians 2:14 NKJV).

> *Yet in all these things we are more than conquerors through Him who loved us* (Romans 8:37 NKJV).

What Jesus endured on the Cross we do not have to bear. The work of redemption was a vicarious work in that Jesus did it for others, not for Himself. Therefore, we can identify with Christ in the victory He obtained and apply it to our life by faith—by believing and confessing who we are in Christ. Although we may have been the victim in some situation, we can still identify with Christ in what He did for us at the Cross. We may go through trouble and trials, but we can declare in the midst of it that we're still victors because of what Christ did for us.

APPLYING CHRIST'S VICTORY TO OUR LIFE

Did Jesus endure the Cross? Did Jesus finish His work in spite of all the suffering He went through? Did Jesus defeat the devil, death, and the grave, rising up in His glory to ascend to the right hand of the Father? The answer to all these questions is a big resounding, "Yes!" How then can we apply the victory of Jesus Christ into our life? The answer is well outlined in the following Scriptures:

> *Seeing then that we have a great High Priest who has passed through the heavens, Jesus the Son of God, let us hold fast our confession. For we do not have a High Priest*

who cannot sympathize with our weaknesses, but was in all points tempted as we are, yet without sin. Let us therefore come boldly to the throne of grace, that we may obtain mercy and find grace to help in time of need (Hebrews 4:14-16 NKJV).

#1: Confess What Jesus Did for Us

There is a time to acknowledge to God that you have hurts, pains, and needs that you need His help to overcome. But that should not be our daily lifestyle. We should confess daily with our mouth what Jesus did for us at Calvary, who we are in Christ, and what the Word of God has promised to us. Continually confessing or speaking what the Word of God says in these three areas will help us more than almost anything else we can do. Confess what God has said in His Word rather than speaking about our failures, hurts, feelings, or experiences.

Some people add to or prolong their hurt by continually talking negatively about how bad it hurts and how unfair life has been to them. Although a person may feel like they unloaded when they do that, the truth is they have just re-lived the painful experiences of the past. In fact, by continually talking about it they often increase the size of the hurt in their mind. The best thing a person can do is to keep saying what the Word of God says about them rather than just talking about their problems. By doing this, many of their problems would be solved, and many of the hurts would be healed.

By our words we either identify ourselves with Christ and what He did for us or we identify with our problems. Who we are and what we have in Christ is greater than any problem we're going through. There are many Scriptures, especially in the letters written by the apostle Paul, that tell us who we are in Christ. This is our real identity as Christians and it is through our confession of these Scriptures that we will walk in the reality of it.

For example, 2 Corinthians 5:17 (NKJV) tells us, *"Therefore, if anyone is in Christ, he is a new creation; old things have passed away; behold, all things have become new."* We need to daily confess we are a new creation in Christ, that old things are passed away, and now we're living a new life in Christ Jesus. This affects every area of our life—spirit, soul, and body.

#2: Realize Jesus Is Our High Priest

We should realize Jesus is our High Priest, and He identifies with what we're experiencing as we go through life. We can always come to Him with our problems. He understands our problems, because He endured much worse than we ever will. Jesus Himself is interceding and praying for us. He will stand by us, strengthen us, and see us through every difficulty and every temptation.

Jesus has sent the Holy Spirit to guide us into the Word of God so we can know what Jesus did for us and what He will do for us as our High Priest (see John 16:13-15). He will reveal a New Covenant that offers love instead of judgment, mercy instead of requiring sacrifice, and grace instead of the law.

God's love, mercy, and grace are infinitely more than all the sins, hurts, wounds, sorrows, and griefs of humankind. The Holy Spirit convicts us to come to the throne of grace where Jesus, our High Priest, is now extending the scepter of love, grace, and mercy to grant forgiveness and healing for all.

#3: Come Boldly to the Throne of Grace

At the throne of grace, we can find mercy and help in time of need. But someone might say, "What happened was my fault. I'm in this condition because of what I did. I don't deserve any help. I'm not sure God will heal me because I messed up too badly."

That may be true, but notice what God told us to do—come to the throne of grace! The seat of unmerited favor! The place of acceptance! We may not deserve it, but God has extended His grace toward us anyway. If we received on the basis of what we deserve, it would no longer be given to us by the grace of God. In ourselves we deserve nothing. The apostle Paul said before we were born again, we were strangers to the promises of God, meaning we were not entitled to them. Yet God in His mercy through Jesus at the Cross has made it possible for us to receive His promises.

This means we do not come to God for help based on our own works or values; we come to God based on the work of Jesus at Calvary. We can never approach God on the basis of our worthiness or works. If we could ever come to God based on what we have done, then there would have been no need for Jesus to suffer and die for us at the Cross. We come based upon the punishment and sin He bore for us on the Cross. His suffering has opened the door for our healing and well-being.

JESUS CAME FOR OUR BENEFIT

Jesus did not need the victory at Calvary for Himself; Jesus was living in victory before He ever came to the earth. Throughout His earthly life, Jesus remained the Sinless One, overcoming every temptation and evil that satan hurled at Him. Only at His crucifixion were the sins of the world laid upon Jesus so that the victory He obtained at Calvary could be for us! Now we're to use our faith to lay hold of that victory, healing, deliverance, safety, and well-being for ourselves in Jesus' name.

Before we came to the throne of grace for help, we may have been bothered by *"every weight, and the sin which so easily ensnares us"* (Hebrews 12:1 NKJV). But after we have received His grace and strength, the weight is gone, and the sin that so easily beset us can no longer do so. We may have come to the throne of grace with sickness and disease in our body, but we can go away from the throne of grace having received the healing that Jesus provided for us at Calvary. We may come to God discouraged, depressed, and having no hope. Maybe we've been rejected and betrayed and suffered bitterness and loneliness. But after we receive grace and forgiveness, we can go our way rejoicing because Jesus has obtained the victory for us.

Jesus endured the worst persecution, trials, pain, trouble, and suffering that any person could endure. He was tortured physically, tormented emotionally and mentally in the worst way, and suffered the horrible pains of rejection, condemnation, shame, sin, and death. I'm sure He wondered if it would ever end. No doubt things looked dark and hopeless to Him in the midst of the intense pain and suffering. But the time came when it was over, and He arose and ascended victoriously into Heaven to sit at the seat of honor beside His Father!

TAKE HOLD OF JESUS' HEALING TOUCH

Today, we too may have endured pain and trials beyond what we ever imagined we would. Life may have been more unfair and more hurtful than we had anticipated. There are times when we feel we have reached the bottom of the pit of despair and hopelessness. We may wonder if we can make it. Questions pound our mind like, "Will it be this way the rest of my life? Will there ever be a day without pain, suffering, sorrow, or rejection?"

No matter what has happened, we must learn to come quickly to the throne of grace and allow Jesus our High Priest to bring His healing touch to our life, our body, and our soul. When we do, then we can let go of what happened and rise up out of the ash heaps of yesterday's troubles and sorrows.

This is the hour when we can use our faith to take hold of Jesus' healing hand and allow Him to strengthen us physically and emotionally to walk in a new dimension of life and victory again.

CHAPTER 11

THINKING GOD'S WAY

"Unless we get God's Word in us, our thoughts will continue to reflect the world around us."

In my growing up years, whenever someone didn't understand something they would often say, "God works in mysterious ways His wonders to perform." Usually people said that after something bad happened. Hearing that gave me the idea that as mere humans we can't figure out what God will do in any given situation. That also led me to think that whatever happens must be God's will because He is the only one who knows what should be done.

But I read in the newspapers about evil and suffering of every kind in the world. People around me were sick, grieving over lost loved ones, and struggling with great difficulties or tragedies in life. I became greatly disillusioned with God who didn't seem to care or give any guarantees in life. I hoped for the best but often thought if God had anything to do with my future it probably wouldn't be good.

Many people think we can't know how God thinks. I visited with a person who told me in the denomination he grew up in they emphasized that God is sovereign and all-knowing; therefore, He can do whatever He wants to do at any time. He can be good or bad, kind or cruel, merciful or judgmental at His sovereign discretion. Consequently, this man found it hard to depend on God for the help he needed.

ACKNOWLEDGE GOD'S GREATNESS

It is true that God knows a whole lot more than we do. And at times it may seem as if we cannot know what God thinks about a situation or person. Even King Solomon acknowledged that God knew much more than he did when he said, *"Do not be rash with your mouth, and let not your heart utter anything hastily before God. For God is in heaven, and you on earth; therefore let your words be few"* (Ecclesiastes 5:2 NKJV). While we acknowledge God is much smarter than we are, we must avoid the hopeless attitude that it is impossible to know what God's will is for us or know what He wants to do in a certain situation.

God is bigger than we are, and He can do what we can't do. He knows more than we do, and His thoughts are better, greater, and higher than ours. God thinks on a different level than our natural thinking. He has a different perspective than we do about life. Often in the middle of a hopeless situation when our mind is racing and our emotions are high, it's hard to think or believe a solution is possible. But God thinks higher, better, and greater than we do, and He knows how to help us through our situation.

CAN WE DISCOVER GOD'S THOUGHTS?

"For My thoughts are not your thoughts, nor are your ways My ways," says the Lord. "For as the heavens are higher than the earth, so are My ways higher than your ways, and My thoughts than your thoughts" (Isaiah 55:8-9 NKJV).

Oh, the depth of the riches both of the wisdom and knowledge of God! How unsearchable are His judgments and His ways past finding out! (Romans 11:33 NKJV)

Eye has not seen, nor ear heard, nor have entered into the heart of man the things which God has prepared for those who love Him (1 Corinthians 2:9 NKJV).

Some people quote these verses as proof texts that we can't know God's will. They often quote it with a tone of voice implying that God is much greater than man, and therefore it is impossible to know His will. But as is often the case, these verses along with others were pulled out of context and taken to mean something God never intended.

It's true that a natural, sinful person by themselves doesn't think the way God does and they can't walk in God's ways with their natural ability. But even under the Old Covenant, God made His ways known to Moses (see Psalm 103:7), and in the New Covenant we have a better covenant established upon better promises.

God has written His thoughts in a book called the Bible so we can learn them. In our Christian walk, we are on a continual journey to find new thoughts and discover new and better ways that God has of doing things. God wants us to find out as much as we can; that is why He gave us His Word to read and His Spirit to dwell within us. It is possible for believers to know what God is thinking in different situations and what His plans are for our lives.

As believers, we have the Holy Spirit living in us. One of the fundamental tasks of the Holy Spirit is to reveal the Word of God to us, which is the thoughts of God in written form. Thus, we can know the thoughts and ways of God by reading His Word and asking the Holy Spirit to give us understanding of it. It is true that no matter how much we know of God's plans, we certainly haven't exhausted the depths of God's knowledge and wisdom. The best ideas and plans we can come up with on our own don't compare to what God has planned for us.

DISCOVERING THE THINGS OF GOD

In Isaiah 46:10 (NKJV) the prophet shows God *"Declaring the end from the beginning, and from ancient times things that are not yet done, saying, 'My counsel shall stand, and I will do all My pleasure.'"* God is speaking prophetically to Israel about returning from exile in Babylon to their homeland. Although nothing in their natural situation indicated this was possible, yet God assures them His counsel, or His thoughts, shall stand and they will come to pass.

Often God will speak to us in the same way. He tells us something that is going to happen in a different time frame than we're in at the moment. Thus God's thoughts will often far exceed our current level of thinking or planning. God has given us the knowledge in His Word of where both spiritual truths and natural provision can be found.

GOD PUT HIS THOUGHTS IN A BOOK

The apostle Paul went on to say in the following verses:

But God has revealed them to us through His Spirit. For the Spirit searches all things, yes, the deep things of God. For what man knows the things of a man except the spirit of the man which is in him? Even so no one knows the things of God except the Spirit of God. Now we have received, not the spirit of the world, but the Spirit who is from God, that we might know the things that have been freely given to us by God (1 Corinthians 2:10-12 NKJV).

These verses are connected to verse 9, which we looked at previously.

First Corinthians 2:9 is not meant to be interpreted by itself; it only presents part of a truth that is not completed until we read verses 10-12. These verses clearly state that the Holy Spirit will show us what God has prepared for us. Although man by himself with no help cannot possibly know the thoughts of God, yet the Holy Spirit in us reveals God's thoughts to us. Most of the time, the Holy Spirit will direct us to the Word of God to find out what God thinks about humankind, about life, and about different situations.

God has written His thoughts in the Bible so we can know God's thoughts and plans for us. Second Timothy 3:16 (NKJV) tells us that *"All Scripture is given by inspiration of God."* The writers of the Bible often wrote to address specific situations or groups of people, but the Holy Spirit helped them to write, guiding them to write the correct words that accurately revealed God's thoughts. The word *inspiration* means "God-breathed," indicating that the words of the Bible came directly from the mind of God to the minds of men, which they then wrote down. The Bible is full of "God-thoughts" that we can read and believe. As we read and meditate the Word of

God, we open our thinking to embrace God's thoughts that He has written in His Word.

Sometimes people have a mental block about the Bible, thinking since it is such a big book, how can we possibly know what it says? No matter how little we know the Bible, we can start with a daily devotional reading, maintain a teachable mind, and be willing to adjust our thinking to embrace God's thoughts in His Word as we are given understanding. Thinking the thoughts of God doesn't mean we have to know or be able to recall every verse in the Bible, but we should be on a journey of knowing as much as we can.

Most people's thoughts focus on a natural level—on the laws that govern this physical world, on man's philosophies and reasoning, on current events and the state of affairs in our nations, or on their own personal circumstances. These thoughts are on a different level than God's thoughts. So we must take time to renew our minds to the written Word of God until its truths and principles have become the dominant pattern in our thinking. God's thoughts from the Word reveal the level of life that God wants us to live. The Word shows us the things He plans for us to do. As we gain knowledge of the thoughts of God's Word, we can set our affections on things above and flow with the direction God wants us to go.

OUR THINKING CAN GET IN THE WAY

Our human thinking is often our greatest opponent as we read God's Word to learn His thoughts and plans for us. When God speaks to us, He often shares thoughts that are far beyond the thoughts we've been thinking. When a new thought is presented to us, our mind tries to connect it to other existing thought patterns. When the mind can't connect the new thought to any related thoughts that it already has, the reaction of the mind is to reject it as not being true or possible.

For example, our mind may have a hard time seeing how an event that happened 2,000 years ago could affect the destiny of humankind today, but John 3:16 (NKJV) tells us, *"For God so loved the world that He gave His only begotten Son, that whoever believes in Him should not perish but have everlasting life."* This verse presents the eternal thoughts of God on salvation that are still true and applicable to us today.

GOD'S THOUGHTS ABOUT HEALING

Often when most people get sick, their predominant thoughts are on the sickness, what the doctor said, their feelings, the pain and discomfort, how long this will last, and their chances of recovering. Then, when someone tells them that Isaiah 53:5 (NKJV) says, *"By His stripes we are healed,"* they may ask, "But I'm sick. What does 'by His stripes I am healed' have to do with me?" At first their mind may not accept that God provided healing for them through the suffering of Jesus at the Cross as a valid and relevant truth.

When we first hear the truths about healing from Isaiah 53:5 and other Scriptures in the Bible, our mind tries to relate them to other thoughts it has about healing. If no other thoughts on healing exist in our mind, these healing verses may not immediately be accepted as truth. Yet after hearing the truth of these verses a number of times, our mind will eventually begin to think that way and accept them as true and possible for our lives.

GOD'S THOUGHTS ON GIVING

Some people have trouble relating to Malachi 3:10-12 concerning tithing and giving offerings and what God will do in response to a person who obeys Him in this area. Our mind tries to find existing thoughts to which it can connect to this truth. If it can't find any, our mind doesn't instruct us to give tithes and offerings.

In math class at school, we were taught that taking one from ten leaves us nine, which is less than what we started with. But God says if we'll give a tenth from our income, He will multiply what is left until we have more than we had before. It takes repeatedly hearing God's Word for our minds to receive the truth of giving tithes and offerings, which promise a greater harvest than what was given before.

As we continually renew our minds with the Word of God, we are building new files in our minds to think the way God does. After a while, when a truth from God's Word comes into our mind, it searches its existing files and connects the new Bible thoughts with them and now recognizes them as true. This is how we put the thoughts of God into our mind and build thought patterns of thinking the way God does.

MY STORY OF GETTING UNDERSTANDING

As a young Christian, I went through a period of time when it seemed as if I couldn't comprehend anything I read in the Bible. I became very frustrated, and at one point I had almost stopped reading my Bible. One Wednesday evening, I slipped in late to the mid-week service at the little storefront church I was attending and discovered they had a guest speaker whom I had never met.

At the end of his message, the guest speaker said to me by the Spirit, "Young man, I see that you're not reading your Bible because you don't understand it. Don't try to figure out what the Bible means. Your job is to read it and trust the Holy Spirit to reveal it to you."

This revolutionized my Bible reading and opened my thinking to embrace what the Holy Spirit would show me. After that I began to eagerly read the Word of God, expecting the Holy Spirit to illuminate its truths and bring understanding to me.

At that time, I worked in a factory doing things that didn't require a lot of mental concentration. As I worked, I would meditate and confess the Scriptures I had read. Understanding by the Holy Spirit came so freely that frequently I would quickly write down what I had learned.

The Holy Spirit reveals the things of God, both spiritual and material things, to us as we look to Him. As we renew our mind to the Word of God, we'll be able to hear the voice of the Holy Spirit more easily and in a greater measure. God wants us to think supernatural thoughts. What the Holy Spirit will say and do is supernatural and will give us understanding of God's thoughts, plans, and ideas that are at a higher level than we would normally think. He will lead us into the Word of God to show us the thoughts and ways of God so we can enter into a higher realm of flowing with God than ever before.

MOVING WITH THE HOLY SPIRIT

There is a great outpouring of God's Spirit in the earth in these days, and it is happening in a greater measure than ever before. This is what the prophets have foretold. God is looking for people who will cooperate with His Spirit in this present day move—people who want to move with Him, think they can move with Him, and dare to move with Him.

It's important that we renew our mind to God's Word because we will flow with the Holy Spirit according to our thinking and understanding of His truth. We can increase our effectiveness and walk in a greater measure of what the Holy Spirit is doing in these days by renewing our mind with God's Word.

Jesus shared insights about who the Holy Spirit is and what He does in John 14–16, showing that we can know the Person of the Holy Spirit. Jesus said He will send the Holy Spirit to us and we know He did come on the Day of Pentecost. The truth is, He is still here, and He will be here until the return of Jesus Christ to receive His people in the Rapture. Jesus said the Holy Spirit has many tasks, including:

- ▸ Helping us (John 14:16)
- ▸ Always being with us (John 14:16-17)
- ▸ Teaching us (John 14:26)
- ▸ Bringing things to our remembrance (John 14:26)
- ▸ Testifying about Jesus to us (John 15:26)
- ▸ Convicting us of sin, righteousness, and judgment (John 16:8-11)
- ▸ Guiding us (John 16:13)
- ▸ Showing us the future (John 16:13)
- ▸ Declaring and showing us who Jesus is and what He has done for us (John 16:14-15)
- ▸ Empowering us (Acts 1:8)

THE BIGGEST HINDRANCE

As we come to know the Word of God and the Person of the Holy Spirit, our thoughts will reflect the work of God rather than our own efforts. Then we can move in greater dimensions of the supernatural.

Many Christians read about the gifts of the Holy Spirit and long to be used in them. The Holy Spirit wants to move through everyone who will allow Him to do so.

Why are so few Christians being used as vessels through which the gifts and power of the Holy Spirit flow? Obviously, some denominations teach against the Holy Spirit moving in these days, which leads people to think they shouldn't move in these gifts and power of God. On an individual level, primarily people don't operate in these things because they think they can't. They don't think they know enough or they're afraid they'll make a mistake if they try to operate in the gifts of the Spirit.

The biggest hindrance in cooperating with the Holy Spirit is our thinking. Often when God reveals the big plans He has for people, they reject them because of their level of thinking. Our small thinking is not consistent with what God wants to make big in our lives. We show no loyalty to God when we insist on holding on to our little thoughts, especially when He wants to do something big in our lives.

God's thoughts are bigger and better than we would normally think, but God is willing for us to know them. That is why we must become students of God's Word and seekers of Him in prayer. Otherwise, we will sabotage God's plans by allowing our thinking to be locked in on small and insignificant things that are far less than what He wanted.

MORE THAN WE CAN ASK OR THINK

> *Now to Him who is able to do exceedingly abundantly above all that we ask or think, according to the power that works in us* (Ephesians 3:20 NKJV).

Many have the idea that God is sovereign, and He will do what this verse says at His own discretion and pleasure without any input from humankind. Their idea is that if God wants to, He will sovereignly and arbitrarily someway, somehow, sometime do something for us far beyond what we can think or imagine. Too often the Church has passively waited on God, telling each other, *"God is able to do exceedingly, abundantly above what we can think or ask."*

It is absolutely true that God can do much more than we can think or imagine, yet a careful study of this verse tells us how God will typically work in our life. God is *able* to do abundantly above all that we ask or think, but that doesn't mean that He *will* usually do abundantly more for us than we ask or think.

GOD'S POWER WORKS IN US

This verse tells us that God will do *"according to the power that works in you."* Throughout the Scriptures, we see the governing factor determining how much of the power of God that worked in people typically was according to their thinking and their asking. Thinking and believing God's thoughts will enable us to ask for things and speak words in line with His Word, and it raises the level of how much God is able to work effectually in us, through us, and for us.

The Holy Spirit is always listening to what we think and ask. He is waiting for us to speak words that will release Him to work in our life. When we ask according to God's thoughts found in His Word, it allows the Holy Spirit to do great and mighty things in us and move us into new realms of living.

IN GOD'S GLORIOUS PRESENCE

"And I will shake all nations, and they shall come to the Desire of All Nations, and I will fill this temple with glory," says the Lord of hosts. "The silver is Mine, and the gold is Mine," says the Lord of hosts. "The glory of this latter temple shall be greater than the former," says the Lord of hosts. "And in this place I will give peace," says the Lord of hosts (Haggai 2:7-9 NKJV).

These verses speak of God's former glory, which was in the tabernacle and in Solomon's temple, and His glory in the latter temple, which some say is the ideal temple seen by Ezekiel. But, "the latter house" also refers to the believer who is the temple of the Holy Spirit in the New Covenant, where the presence and power of God dwells greater than in the former house.

As we become conscious of the fact that we are the temples of God containing the glory of God, which is His manifest presence and power, it becomes easier for us to think the thoughts of God and ask Him for the right things for our life. Haggai 2:7-9 indicates that God will give us thoughts of plenty and thoughts of peace in His glory, no matter what our current circumstances may be.

A FORETASTE OF HEAVENLY THINGS

In the verses we just read, while talking about His glory God also talks about gold and silver. Some have said this is a picture of Heaven, where there are streets of gold in the midst of the presence of God. That may be true, but this also shows that God wants the life of the believer to be in line with what is already a reality in Heaven.

The life we live as believers here on earth is a foretaste of heavenly things. The Holy Spirit is called the earnest of our inheritance (see Ephesians 1:14 KJV), which actually refers to a down payment of what we'll have in Heaven. Being conscious of the glorious presence of God helps us have a greater understanding of God's abundance. This enables us to move into more and greater things.

CHANGED BY THE SPIRIT OF GOD

> *But we all, with open face beholding as in a glass the glory of the Lord, are changed into the same image from glory to glory, even as by the Spirit of the Lord* (2 Corinthians 3:18 KJV).

This verse indicates a transformation happens as time after time we immerse ourselves in the manifested presence of God's glory. This transformation in our soul usually happens little by little, day by day, as we read God's Word and listen to the Holy Spirit. As we allow God to minister to us, His glory will influence our soul, taking away our old, earthly, worldly thoughts and lifting us into thoughts of His kingdom, power, and glory. There our priorities and affections will change. Things we once thought were important won't be as important to us after spending time in the glory of God.

Jesus' disciples were living testimonies of being transformed into useful and powerful vessels that God used to build His kingdom. What the disciples did after they received the outpouring of the Holy Spirit in Acts 2:1-4 was quite different from what they did in the Gospels. In the book of Acts, the disciples rose up to become fishers of men and world changers. We too can rise up into what

God has for us as we allow the Holy Spirit to change our thoughts, especially during manifestations of God's glorious presence.

EXPERIENCING GOD'S GLORY

Often, the biggest hindrance to flowing with the plan of God is found in our thought life. We usually flow with the Holy Spirit according to our understanding or the knowledge we have. So being in the glory of God becomes invaluable as a change agent for our thought life. Our mind becomes more open to God's plan, and we yield ourselves more readily to what God desires us to do. There we are able to more readily grasp the possibility of a different life from the one we have been living.

The apostle Paul is one of the greatest examples of a person who was changed in the glory of God. His thoughts about the things of God were changed in a moment when the glorious presence of God came upon him on the Damascus road (see Acts 9:3-8). He stopped thinking thoughts of murder, hatred, and persecuting Christians and began to think thoughts about fulfilling the will of God.

WHEN GOD'S PEOPLE GET TOGETHER

The glorious presence and power of God can also manifest in a church setting where the body of believers is gathered. We must not forsake getting together with other believers when church services are available or we will forfeit an opportunity to become who God wants us to be. Some things can only be received in the gathering of God's people as the Holy Spirit ministers in an atmosphere of corporate faith. As people of like faith gather together to worship God in spirit and truth and the revelation of God's written Word is shared, the atmosphere becomes such that God manifests in their midst. God inhabits our praises, for Psalm 9:11 (NKJV) tells us, *"Sing praises to the Lord, who dwells in Zion!"* Zion is a type of the Church, and God is desiring His people to lift their voices in praise to Him. He desires to manifest Himself in a great way in the corporate gathering of His church to transform His people and bring glory to Himself.

CHAPTER 12

BUILDING THOUGHTS OF FAITH

"Building thoughts of faith in our mind and heart helps us to trust in God's big plans, even though we may not totally understand them."

A number of years ago I became very sick, which caused me to be weak, nauseated, and unable to endure bright lights and loud sounds. We did all we could in the natural, but it seemed to no avail. I repeatedly quoted the healing promises in God's Word, but I was struggling with my thoughts. One day these words rose up in my spirit and got my attention: *"Jesus Christ maketh thee whole."* I recognized this short sentence came from Acts 9:34 (KJV), and realized the Holy Spirit had directed me to it. So I began to say this sentence over and over throughout the day to myself. Sometimes thoughts pounded my mind like, "You'll never get well and be able to serve God," or "You're losing your mind. You'll never be normal again." But I kept speaking this sentence over and over as much as necessary to drown out those thoughts of fear and doubt that wanted to take control of my mind. This short sentence became my lifeline that I held on to. I must have spoken this sentence hundreds, maybe thousands of times a day. As I continued to do this day after day, I gradually began to recover, until eventually I returned to full health with no aftereffects.

All too often, in difficult times our thoughts want to go in many directions. Our thoughts often bounce around like a rubber ball, going back and forth from our feelings and emotions to the thoughts we know to be true in our heart. David said, *"Keep my soul, and deliver me; let me not be ashamed, for I put my trust in You"* (Psalm 25:20 NKJV). He needed God to help him because of the trouble he was facing. He asked God for help and then declared he was putting his trust in God.

DON'T LET NEGATIVE THOUGHTS TAKE OVER

There is no more critical time for a person to remain focused in their thinking than in difficult times. I've heard people say, "You can't keep a bird from flying over your head, but you can keep him from building a nest in your hair." The same can be said for our thoughts. Many thoughts come and go in our mind on a daily basis, and our job is to sort out which ones we retain.

An average person will have thousands of thoughts during the course of a single, ordinary day. Our task is to sort through those thoughts and meditate on the right thoughts that help us have faith to get through difficulties, to accomplish our mission, or to reach the next level in life. We can allow negative thoughts to overtake our mind until they lead us into doubt and despair. Or we can develop encouraging, positive thoughts that lead us into faith. Our thoughts either lead us into believing we can do God's will or cause us to hide in unbelief. It is therefore paramount that we gain knowledge of God's Word until that knowledge forms the predominant thoughts in our mind. This creates an alignment between the thoughts in our soul and what we believe in our heart—or spirit, as some people call it.

Developing a prosperous soul in which the mind is renewed to God's Word does not take the place of having faith in our heart or spirit. Rather, it leads us to being able to have strong faith in God's Word. If we entertain thoughts long enough in our mind, eventually they will form into a belief in our heart.

LEARN TO MANAGE OUR THOUGHT LIFE

If we're going to make it through difficulties and trouble or move to another level in life, we have to learn how to manage our thought life so it is aligned with the Word of God that we believe in our heart. As we meditate on the Scriptures, eventually they will become our most dominant thoughts and the Holy Spirit will write them on the tablets of our heart (see 2 Corinthians 3:3).

Years ago, the person who bought our house on contract for deed stopped making the monthly payments. That meant we didn't have the money to make the mortgage payment on the house, and unless something major happened it looked like we would have to file for bankruptcy. We advertised the house to sell it, but the bank that held the mortgage kept threatening to foreclose on the house.

I continued daily and weekly communicating with the bank, asking them to give me time to sell the house and reminding them it was cheaper for them to give me time to sell it than it would be to hire attorneys to foreclose on the house. I also went to the Word of God and found a verse of Scripture dealing with our situation and began confessing it over and over, as often as I thought about it (which was numerous times a day)!

It took about four months to sell the house, and during that entire time my mind was racing with negative thoughts of losing everything and going under. In my heart I believed what the Scriptures said about God taking care of us until this situation was over, but in my mind I was being pounded with all kinds of doubtful and fearful thoughts. But I kept reading and speaking that verse of Scripture over and over to my situation, making the truths of that verse a part of my thoughts. Eventually the thoughts of fear and doubt began to diminish and I began to think more consistently in line with the verse I believed in my heart.

HARMONY BETWEEN SOUL AND SPIRIT

So our human spirit can be enlightened on the things of God without our soul having much understanding of how it can be possible. A person can have faith in their heart and doubt in their mind. In times of tragedy, trouble, or adversity, many conflicting thoughts try to crowd into our minds. But we must keep feeding on the Word of God so we can sort through our thoughts and select the ones we want to keep. While a person may be in this condition, it certainly isn't God's best. God desires that our soul and spirit to be in agreement and have knowledge and understanding of the things of God.

God desires our soul and spirit to be in harmony with His Word. This means that our thoughts and our beliefs should be in agreement with each other as much as possible. The Holy Spirit wants to enlighten both our spirit and our soul by the Word of God. Our spirit receives revelation from the Holy Spirit, while our soul is

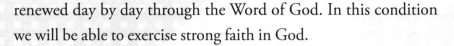

renewed day by day through the Word of God. In this condition we will be able to exercise strong faith in God.

God desires our spirit and our soul to be in agreement by having the same understanding of truth. For example, we must become fully persuaded that our sicknesses and diseases were laid on Christ. Then our mind and our heart can come into total agreement and healing is inevitable. This is true not only about receiving healing but in receiving whatever else we need from God.

KNOWING GOD'S WORD PRODUCES FAITH

Our soul is the "gate" to our heart; the knowledge in our soul that we actively dwell upon will eventually enter into our heart and cause us to believe. Keep in mind that thoughts of God's Word come into our mind before they create faith in our heart. The value of a prosperous soul can be experienced when perfect harmony exists between soul and spirit because they have both been enlightened according to the Word of God. Then we can experience peace and express great faith in God's Word.

Romans 10:17 (NKJV) states that, *"Faith comes by hearing, and hearing by the word of God."* As we fill our mind with the knowledge of God's Word, the Holy Spirit will begin to write the Word upon our heart. When the Holy Spirit engraves the Word upon our heart, it creates faith in God. Our ability to have faith in our heart concerning the Word of God is in direct proportion to the knowledge we have of God's Word.

Often what we think in our mind will lead to what we believe in our heart, and what we believe will influence what we say out of our mouth. It all begins with what we choose to think. Thinking thoughts according to God's Word is the correct foundation for our faith in God.

If we're constantly thinking according to the world's way of doing things, we're laying a foundation for doubt and fear. At some point the pressures of life will cause our incorrect foundation of "worldly thinking" to crumble, and our faith will not be strong enough to withstand the adversities of life and the attacks of the enemy.

MORE THAN POSITIVE MENTAL ATTITUDE

I am not referring to mere mental assent or positive thinking. Just thinking the right thoughts in your mind is not enough, nor is it an end in itself. Some people think that knowledge is all they need, but if that were true then knowledge would be their savior. The reason we must have knowledge from God's Word is because it is the thoughts of God that enable us to believe correctly in our hearts.

Some religious people get upset with people who promote having a positive mental attitude. But stop and think about it—God doesn't want us to have negative attitudes. God always responds positively toward believers. Romans 8:32 tells us that God is for us, not against us. Even when we make mistakes or sin, God still leads us to repentance so we can return to Him. Negative thinking shouldn't be an option for us. The truth is, having a positive mental attitude is necessary and good as far as it goes, but there is more to receiving from God than just that.

The value of positive mental attitude is that it is in agreement with the promise of God's Word that we must believe in our heart so we can receive from God (see Mark 11:23-24). We may never see the results of believing with our heart unless we work to bring the attitudes of our mind into agreement with the Word of God.

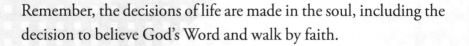

Remember, the decisions of life are made in the soul, including the decision to believe God's Word and walk by faith.

DOUBT CAN BE DEVASTATING

Years ago, I accepted the pastorate of a small denominational church seventeen miles out in the country. In the congregation was a farmer who was having great financial difficulties and his farm was about to go into bankruptcy. This situation had worked on him until he was depressed and in despair. As I visited with him, I shared how God's promises are for us today and how God has promised in His Word to help us. After talking with him for a while, I asked him if we can pray for God to help him with his finances and make a way for him to keep his farm. But he slowly shook his head and said, "No, I think that whatever happens is the will of God."

What he said revealed what he had been taught and the ideas about God that he had embraced into his thought life and belief system. Consequently, this was how he looked at life and determined his actions. Because of the way this man thought, he decided that prayer would not help his situation. Eventually, the farmer lost his farm in bankruptcy without giving God a chance to do anything for him.

DECIDE TO THINK THOUGHTS OF FAITH

We must learn to think God's thoughts. God always thinks thoughts in agreement with His Word. More specifically, God thinks thoughts of faith and love. God always thinks *"with God all things are possible"* (Mark 10:27 NKJV). He thinks conquering thoughts of victory and not thoughts of defeat. He thinks about healing, protection, and provision for His people. God thinks about the harvest of souls and bringing the message of salvation to the world.

If we want to move to another level of life or take the next step in God's plan for our life, we must decide to think thoughts from God's Word. We must guard our thought life so that only thoughts of faith in God are dominant in our soul. We cannot afford to play around with thoughts that are contrary to God's Word; we must be quick to reject thoughts that do not express faith.

IDENTIFY THOUGHTS OF DOUBT AND FAITH

Some time ago, someone gave me a copy of a message by a speaker they thought was wonderful. I had heard that speaker was really good, and so I eagerly began to listen to the message. I waited for several minutes to hear him say something that would build me up and strengthen my faith, but instead he was talking negatively and with a doom and gloom outlook. Suddenly, this particular thought came up out of my heart to my conscious mind, and I spoke it out loud: "This message is not building my faith." I immediately discontinued listening to it. I refuse to allow thoughts of doubt that are contrary to faith in God's Word to occupy my mind. I sometimes tell people, "I worked too hard for the faith I have to allow other people to rob me with their thoughts of doubt and unbelief."

Many Christians have not filled their minds and hearts with God's thoughts. Therefore, they have a difficult time believing God's Word. They waver between thoughts of God's Word and thoughts of this world. They want to believe the Word, but they have not taken the time to put the Word in them sufficiently until the Word becomes their predominant thought. Their mind and heart are still moved by what goes on around them.

God wants our mind and heart to be filled with His thoughts from His Word that tell us all things are possible. Often our first challenge is to conquer and take control of our mind, and then we are in position to conquer the mountains of difficulties and impossibilities that stand in our way. We must continually dwell upon God's Word that says we are a conqueror in life. When the challenges of life come, those possibility thoughts and conquering thoughts we have been putting in our soul and heart will rise up and govern our steps. They will guide us to victory. They will enable us to see God's promises come to pass.

MEDITATE UPON THE WORD OF GOD

As we meditate upon the promises of God in our soul and spirit, eventually they will rise up strong within us. Then a spirit of faith will rise up in us that will not be denied. A spirit of faith declares it is possible to conquer the mountains that appear in our life. Trouble may come, and storm clouds may appear on the horizon, but they are no match for the spirit of faith that rises up on the inside of us.

The spirit or attitude of faith dares to think, believe, and speak the Word of God no matter what it may look like. A person whose mind is convinced and they fully believe with their heart what God has promised to them will boldly march into the face of impossibilities, declaring nothing is too difficult or too big to accomplish or overcome.

As we begin to let the possibilities of God dwell richly in us, Scriptures like *"with God all things are possible"* (Mark 10:27 NKJV) will become real to us. That is why we must meditate upon the truth and the possibility that all things are possible for us. Continually ponder or meditate on the truth that in God there is no defeat or failure. Begin to imagine God working all things for your good (see Romans 8:28).

BELIEVE ALL THINGS ARE POSSIBLE

Jesus said, *"If you can believe, all things are possible to him who believes"* (Mark 9:23 NKJV). When the angel told Mary that she would conceive by the Holy Spirit and that she would give birth to the Son of God, her response was not one of unbelief. Although she did not fully understand in her mind how this would be possible, she immediately responded, *"Let it be to me according to your word"* (Luke 1:38 NKJV).

If we're going to move forward in God's plan and get through the difficulties of life, we must decide that whether or not we completely understand how the Word of God can happen in our lives, our immediate response will be, "Be it unto me according to Your Word." Then we must take the things God has spoken to us and begin to ponder them in our heart and mind.

We must meditate upon them until the revelation of God's Word comes to us. At that point we can rise up in faith to accomplish in the power of the Holy Spirit what the Word has spoken to us. Then God will see our faith and say to us, *"Be it unto you according to your faith!"*

WE MUST GUARD OUR THOUGHTS

It is very difficult to maintain a strong confession of faith while continually thinking thoughts of doubt, fear, and confusion. We must learn to control our thoughts by continually feeding on new thoughts from God's Word. What we constantly listen to or look at will eventually become the dominant thoughts in our mind and imaginations. Reading the Word or listening to messages that help build our faith is necessary if we want to continually speak and act according to God's plan.

We can't allow our mind to have the option of thinking and replaying any old negative thoughts that come along and then expect to be able to declare God's promises in the time of crisis. What we have put in our mind and heart will inevitably come out of our mouth when the pressures of life come our way.

It is imperative that we assign guards around our mind so we think thoughts from God's Word instead of dwelling on our problems or the various opinions of others. Whenever we face a crisis or difficulty, other well-meaning people will often offer reasonable alternatives to obeying God's Word that may seem easier to do, have less risk, or be more acceptable to others. No doubt most of them are well-meaning people, and what some will say has some wisdom that we may be able to use.

But we must learn to deflect ideas that are contrary to the Word of God and not allow them to take root in our thought life. Speaking the truth of God's Word will help us when nothing else can; that's why we must hold on to His Word in spite of everything else.

We must learn to do what Paul told Timothy, a young preacher who was about to take over the pastorate at the church of Ephesus: *"Timothy, guard the Good News which has been entrusted to you. Turn away from pointless discussions and the claims of false knowledge that people use to oppose the Christian faith"* (1 Timothy 6:20 GW).

The church at Ephesus had numerous false teachers in it who wanted to persuade people to follow them instead of following God. No doubt they wanted to convince Timothy to follow them instead of following Christ and what He had accomplished at the Cross.

So Timothy had to guard his thought life and fortify his mind by not listening to their erroneous ideas, and instead continually meditate—think and talk—on God's Word and on Christ's redemptive work at the Cross. It isn't always easy to fend off the ideas of others and stay focused on the promises of God's Word, but doing so will help us stay on the road to victory.

FILL UP WITH GOD'S WORD

Some people have difficulty maintaining a consistent confession of what the Word has promised them. This is caused by either not controlling their thought lives or not listening to the Word of God enough until they believe it. Jesus said, *"out of the abundance of the heart his mouth speaks"* (Luke 6:45). The Twentieth Century New Testament says it this way, *"what fills a man's heart will rise to his lips."* God designed us to speak words of faith that rise up out of the abundance, or overflow, of the Word that is in our heart. Sadly, most people don't have the Word of God in them in abundance; they only have enough to barely get by in life. Therefore, the Word does not overflow out of their heart and come out of their mouth in time of need or when they're dealing with the pressures of life.

I know there are crisis times in our lives when our minds are overwhelmed and seem to go into shock. In moments like these, it takes great effort to think thoughts of believing that God will help us or to keep on speaking words of faith. That's why we need to learn how to control our thoughts and feed upon the Word of God when there is no crisis in our life.

DECIDE TO DISCOVER GOD'S THOUGHTS

We shouldn't wait for trouble to come knocking on our door before we decide to control our thoughts and listen to the Word. That's like trying to fix the dam after it breaks and the water has already started flowing over it. Realize that we must get our thinking right so that we can believe right, and then what we continually say will be right. It all begins with thinking on the right things. Eventually, as we think, believe, and speak the Word, then we'll be able to receive what we need from God.

CHAPTER 13

MOVING UP TO THE NEXT LEVEL

"Our thoughts in the past have brought us into the present world; our thoughts today will also help us step into our future."

I talked with a man named Joe who grew up in a very strict religious family on a farm. One day when Joe was seventeen years old, he decided to leave the farm. Someone told him about another farmer who needed help, and he worked for him for several weeks. After that Joe heard about a farmer in another community who needed help, so Joe decided to work for him. This farmer was on the school board, and he asked Joe if he wanted to go to high school. So Joe decided to go to high school. Upon graduation, he decided to go into the military where he served for four years. After that, Joe decided to have a career in banking, which he did successfully until he retired. After retiring, he and his wife decided to enroll in a Bible college and graduated two years later. Today, Joe is a Christian serving faithfully in his church. The decisions Joe made allowed God to help him move from one level to the next in life.

Every day people go to their jobs, vocations, and professions—some make great advancements in life and break into new levels of life and achievements, while others remain locked into the life they're now living and see no opportunity to better themselves or advance to a higher paying job. Many are aware that higher and better realms of living exist but often don't know how to get there. Others start their life with lofty and worthy dreams and end up doing something far less because it pays the bills. Their dreams remain deep down inside, and as time goes on their dreams grow dim as they think less and less about them.

GOD HAS MADE A WAY

The truth is that God has made a way for people to rise up in life, moving from one level of life to another. God Himself lives in a realm higher than the physical realm that humanity lives within. Yet He has sent His Son to die for humankind, making it possible for us to rise from a sinful life into a life of righteousness and holiness, to move from the darkness of the past into the brightness of God's promises.

> "For My thoughts are not your thoughts, nor are your ways My ways," says the Lord. "For as the heavens are higher than the earth, so are My ways higher than your ways, and My thoughts than your thoughts" (Isaiah 55:8-9 NKJV).

God's thoughts are not only different but also higher than human thoughts because they are from a different realm. They reflect the spirit realm of God, which has greater powers and higher purposes than humankind has in the earthly realm in which they live. However, when we know what God's Word says about a certain situation, we know His thoughts about it, for His thoughts are always in agreement with His Word.

EVERY LEVEL HAS ITS OWN THOUGHTS

One day as I was meditating on the Word, this truth became evident to me: "Every realm has its own thoughts." God's realm—the spirit realm—has thoughts according to His Word. The human realm has thoughts dictated by the limitations of its physical environment of the earth. This helps us understand why the natural man in the world doesn't understand the things of God. The apostle Paul said, *"But the natural man does not receive the things of the Spirit of God, for they are foolishness to him; nor can he know them, because they are spiritually discerned"* (1 Corinthians 2:14 NKJV). The natural man and God live in two different realms and thus they think differently.

DIFFERENT LEVELS OF LIFE SURROUND US

Even in the world we live in, there are different realms and levels of life. People in different professions and vocations must have certain knowledge and thinking to be successful and complete their required assignments and tasks. People in different geographical locations think and act differently. Poor people don't understand riches. Chronically sick people often don't comprehend the realm of health. Often there is conflict between employers and employees. When people are in different realms, they each have their own thoughts suited to the way they live and work.

Racial problems have their roots in this fact. This doesn't mean that any particular race is better than another, but they do think differently. One person said, "One of the signs of maturity in Christ is that you can appreciate the diversity of people who are under the common cause of Christ." We can recognize our differences and still be unified and work together under the banner of Jesus Christ.

We need to know that satan tries to work in people's minds to magnify the different thoughts people have to create division, conflict, chaos, violence, crime, and corruption among them. Satan and his realm are full of demonic, evil thoughts that are against God, humanity, and all that is good. Jesus said satan is a liar and a murderer (see John 8:44) and he comes to fulfill his evil agenda to steal, kill, and destroy (see John 10:10). He whispers lies into the minds of people trying to get them to yield to the thoughts of his realm.

THOUGHTS OF THE PAST CAN HOLD YOU CAPTIVE

A number of years ago, I was in a former communist country in Eastern Europe that had just changed over to a democratic government. While they were under communist rule, the government dictated how the people lived and functioned, but under the new democratic government these same people were now free to make their own choices.

Yet the attitudes and ways of many of these people who were now under democratic rule still reflected the laws and regulations of the former communist government. Why was this? Every realm has its own thoughts. A communist government and a democratic society are two different realms, and people in each one think differently. In order for these people in this Eastern European country to change their lifestyle, they had to embrace a major mind shift or change of thinking.

Even though they were now essentially free to live a different way, many were not yet able to function successfully in this new environment. They didn't do well in making their own choices regarding where to live, their professions, activities, and lifestyles. In order to experience the freedom that now belonged to them, they had to go through the process of adopting the thoughts of their new realm.

THE FIRST STEP TO THE NEXT LEVEL

The first step in going to another level or realm is to begin thinking the thoughts of that level or realm. A person must be enlightened according to the thoughts of the realm they want to function in. This is true no matter what realm a person wants to enter into or in which they want to work.

I remember as a young boy living on the farm, every day we got up early to do chores, plant and harvest crops, bale the hay and put it in the barn, and take care of the animals. It was a good life. But the farm was beside a county highway, and every day I watched the cars and trucks go by and wondered where they were all going. I wanted to find out and dreamed of living a life beyond the farm. I thought about living on my own place, imagined driving my own car, and having a job. What I didn't know at that time was that every person's life journey begins with thinking thoughts of the place they want to go.

A friend of mine who was an artist in New York City told me he could always tell who was new in the city, because they were always looking up at the tall buildings! These newcomers were in an environment or culture that was new to them and did not really know the thoughts of people in that realm. So they acted differently than those who already lived and worked there.

THINK GOD'S WORD FOR THE NEXT LEVEL

As we receive God's thoughts from His Word, the Holy Spirit will begin to change our thinking. As we continue to imagine and meditate on the thoughts of another level or realm, we will begin to comprehend its benefits, and a desire to go there will begin to stir within our soul. Eventually, as we keep those thoughts in the forefront of our mind, we'll be able to believe them, say them, and do them.

It is true that rich people think differently than poor people do. Therefore, if we want to go from poverty to prosperity we must learn the thoughts of the realm of prosperity. Unless we change our thought patterns and the level of the knowledge we have about money and financial principles, we'll never rise to a higher level of wealth than where we are right now.

Even if we receive a large sum of money, in some way we will eventually return to the same financial condition we were in before unless we change our thinking about money. Remember, the decisions of life, including what to do with money, are made in the soul. The ability to keep and use money wisely comes with thinking the right thoughts concerning prosperity. Then the money that comes to us will be a blessing, and we can be a blessing to others.

THINK GOD'S WORD FOR IMPROVED HEALTH

Doctors tell some people who are sick that they must change their diet and way of life in order to be physically healthy. For those people to consistently follow the doctor's orders, they must make thoughts about eating healthy and regular exercise a priority in their mind. Even when receiving divine healing, a sick person must change their thoughts by habitually dwelling upon the healing promises of God's

Word. This helps them to believe and speak the promises of God on a consistent basis until they receive their healing.

Many people are not healed because they never take the time to change their thoughts to what God's Word reveals about healing. It is possible for a person to be ignorant of the thoughts in the realm of divine healing and still receive healing through a special manifestation of the Holy Spirit. But that person may not know enough to stay healthy if the devil tries to steal from them. For a person to consistently enjoy health and healing year after year, they must change their thinking so that it agrees with God's healing promises.

THINK GOD'S WORD FOR BUSINESS SUCCESS

In the realm of business, we often find employees and employers at odds with each other. The primary reason for this conflict is in the way they think. For employees to enter into a management position or become an employer, they must have a change of thinking. When they embrace new thoughts of where they want to go, then they are able to move into a different realm than before.

Employees must make the adjustment in their thought lives from being followers to becoming managers or leaders. They must change from dealing with daily tasks to thinking and planning for the future of the company. They must change from only considering what is good on an individual basis to focusing on what is good for everyone as well as the future well-being of the company.

THE ISRAELITES GO TO THE PROMISED LAND

When the Israelites were in the wilderness on the way to the Promised Land, God humbled and proved them so they could know what was in their hearts (see Deuteronomy 8:1-2). God had to change their hearts and minds to His way of thinking in order for them to be able to possess the Promised Land. It took time for God to change their mentality from being slaves to being conquerors—to having a "with God it's possible to conquer" mentality to possess and conquer a land.

We have to think bigger thoughts than the land we want to possess or the new realms we want to enter into. It is impossible for us to enter into a new level of living when the thoughts of that level overwhelm us. The basic meaning of being overwhelmed is to become passive, languish, or even to go hide. This gives a picture of a person who is overwhelmed being reduced to a state of inactivity, even hiding themselves from things or people who try to intimidate or attack them. The devil will try to overwhelm us with a barrage of thoughts to keep us from accomplishing much of anything. He knows if he can win the battle in our mind, the real battle of possessing what God has promised to us in His Word will not happen.

When the twelve Israelite spies went into the Promised Land, ten of them were overwhelmed—not by the inhabitants of the land but by their own thoughts of possessing the land. Their own thoughts defeated them, and they drew back from possessing the land. Except for Joshua and Caleb, the first generation of Israelites who were twenty years and older did not make the adjustment in their thinking from being overwhelmed to believing that, with God, possessing the land was possible. Often the greatest battles in life are fought in our soul—that is where the battles are fought to consistently think the right thoughts. If we can win the battle of our thoughts, then winning the battle to possess God's promises is much easier.

In Joshua 1:1-9, Joshua receives instructions from God to lead the Israelites into the Promised Land. Focusing on his God-given purpose gives him the courage he needs to rise up and lead the nation of Israel into their Promised Land. Three times God tells Joshua *"be strong and of good courage"* (Joshua 1:6,7,9 NKJV). Not only do we need physical strength to possess the promises of God and move to a new level in life, we also need courage in our heart and mind. Most people quit and never enter into what God has for them, not because of their lack of physical strength but because of a lack of courage.

If we listen to God's Word and His Spirit, we can think courageously. In the midst of a great storm that threatened their lives, an angel brought a message from God to Paul assuring him that he would make it through the storm. Whereupon Paul told the rest of the people the message and then declared, *"So take courage! For I believe God! It will be just as he said!"* (Acts 27:25 TLB). When God speaks to us, it gives us the right thoughts in our mind to act with great courage against all odds.

THINKING ABOUT OUR PURPOSE

People often faint and quit because they have no cause or purpose. Or they have forgotten their purpose and instead are continually focused on their circumstances or their adversaries until fear grips their mind and heart. Our purpose in life should always line up with God's Word and His will for our lives. So we must learn to listen to what God speaks to us during times of prayer and reading the Word.

As we meditate upon the things God puts in our heart, plans and strategies will rise up in our thoughts. It is only when a cause or purpose burns strong within our heart and mind that we'll rise up with courage and boldness to do it. This courage provides the inner fuel to move into action to go into a new realm.

COMPREHEND NEW LEVELS OF LIVING

Because every realm has its own thoughts, often it is difficult for us to comprehend how much better the next level is than the one we're living in now. That's why it's often hard for us to move from one level of living to another. Sometimes we get a brief glimpse in our mind of what God desires us to do. But we will only obtain it if we continually hold on to that picture and meditate on the possibility of going there.

Sometimes we don't see the possibilities or opportunities that actually exist around us, especially if they are in another realm or level than what we're living in. It was difficult for the Israelites to possess the Promised Land because they had difficulty conceiving in their minds the possibilities, the benefits, and the privileges of transitioning from living in the wilderness to go into the Promised Land.

On the other hand, David was a person who reminded himself of the benefits of serving God and went from a young shepherd boy to becoming the king of Israel. He told himself, *"Bless the Lord, O my soul, and forget not all His benefits"* (Psalm 103:2 NKJV). He continually kept the benefits of serving God in his thought life as he moved from one level of life to another.

A man was driving around in very rich neighborhood. He drove by a large, fabulous mansion and commented, "I can't imagine living in a mansion like that." Immediately, the Holy Spirit spoke up on the inside of him and said, "Then you'll never have it." Later this man made the comment, "You cannot possess what you cannot imagine."

Changing our lifestyle and way of doing things begins with changing the thoughts and imaginations in our mind to God's way of thinking. This causes our entire approach to life to change. If we're willing to leave our old thoughts and develop new thought patterns of where God wants us to go, we'll eventually rise up to a new level of thinking and living.

REMOVING THE VEIL OF BLINDNESS

Some people have a veil of blindness concerning certain truths in the Word of God. Various things can cause people to be blinded to God's Word, including tradition, erroneous teaching, experiences in life, and sin. Satan himself blinds people's minds to keep them from receiving salvation (see 2 Corinthians 4:4). Paul said concerning the Jews that there was a veil over their minds, which is why they did not recognize the Messiah (see 2 Corinthians 3:15-18).

In the Jewish temple there was a great curtain that separated the Holy Place, or Holy of Holies, from the Inner Court of the temple. This curtain separated the people who were not born again from the presence of God. During the redemptive work of Christ on the Cross, that curtain was torn from top to bottom, opening up the way of understanding and receiving salvation for all humankind.

Today, many who have received Christ in their hearts have not had the veil of natural thinking removed from their minds concerning their rights and privileges in Christ. They are born again but they have never spent time meditating on the Word of God until their thoughts are changed. It takes the truth of God's Word presented to our minds and hearts and the power of the Holy Spirit to tear down the curtain between our old way of thinking and God's way of thinking.

BREAKTHROUGH ON MY JOB

Soon after I was appointed the dean of a small Bible school, I struggled with the administrative and logistical duties of that position. One day in frustration I told God, "Please find someone else to be the dean. Just let me be an instructor, and I'll teach the Word, because I don't have the administrative abilities that this job requires."

Immediately I heard the Lord whisper quietly to my heart, "I look at you as a good administrator." That new thought was a great gift that dropped down inside of me. With that new thought from God, I was able to be successful in that role of being the dean of the Bible school.

EMBRACE NEW THOUGHTS FROM GOD

For I know the thoughts that I think toward you, says the Lord, thoughts of peace and not of evil, to give you a future and a hope. Then you will call upon Me and go and pray to Me, and I will listen to you. And you will seek Me and find Me, when you search for Me with all your heart. I will be found by you, says the Lord, and I will bring you back from your captivity; I will gather you from all the nations and from all the places where I have driven you, says the Lord, and I will bring you to the place from which I cause you to be carried away captive (Jeremiah 29:11-14 NKJV).

Here God spoke to the Israelites through His prophet to reveal His thoughts to them. They had been deported from their homeland and made captives in Babylon because of their wickedness, disobedience, and idolatry. Yet God stated His thoughts about them to show how He looked upon them and what He had planned for their future. He declared thoughts of peace toward them.

While they were still in captivity in Babylon, God saw them with hearts turned toward Him. He said if they would seek Him they would find Him. He promised restoration instead of total judgment. God wanted the outcome of the Israelites to be according to His promises in His covenant with them.

God wants our future to be what His Word promises us. He has already mapped out a success plan for us in His Word, and He expects His Word to be our outcome in life. As we read the Word, we must expect God to unveil our future. Then, as we follow the Word of God, we can make our way through the difficulties and trials that come our way. We'll have a life of peace and not evil, and we'll have an expected outcome.

SEEING THINGS IN OUR FUTURE

Making mention of you in my prayers: that the God of our Lord Jesus Christ, the Father of glory, may give to you the spirit of wisdom and revelation in the knowledge of Him, the eyes of your understanding being enlightened; that you may know what is the hope of His calling, what are the riches of the glory of His inheritance in the saints, and what is the exceeding greatness of His power toward us who believe, according to the working of His mighty power (Ephesians 1:16-19 NKJV).

Most people, like those Paul wrote to in this letter, are clueless about the will of God for their lives. It is a mystery to them. But Paul prayed for the Ephesian believers to have a *spirit of wisdom and revelation* so their understanding would be enlightened concerning

God's will. This is a good prayer for us to pray over ourselves on a daily basis. Psalm 18:28 (NKJV) tells us, *"For You will light my lamp; the Lord my God will enlighten my darkness."* God wants to enlighten us so that we are not in the dark concerning His will.

We should pray Paul's prayer in Ephesians 1:16-18 on a daily basis. Without regular times of prayer, we will not be enlightened concerning God's will for our life. As we ask God for the spirit of wisdom and revelation to show us His will, then our heart will be flooded with light, or knowledge, so that we may know His thoughts concerning our lives.

The Living Bible translates Ephesians 1:18 this way: *"I pray that your hearts will be flooded with light so that you can see something of the future he has called you to share."* God wants His promises to be a part of our future. Therefore, our future does not have to be a mystery to us. As we allow God to give us a revelation from His Word of His realm, we can know who He is, what He has, and what He wants for us.

If we will seek God's face, He will begin to share His thoughts with us and even show us what is going to happen. Jeremiah 33:3 (NKJV) instructs us to, *"Call to Me, and I will answer you, and show you great and mighty things, which you do not know."* Also, Jesus said, *"However, when He, the Spirit of truth, has come, He will guide you into all truth; for He will not speak on His own authority, but whatever He hears He will speak; and He will tell you things to come"* (John 16:13 NKJV).

DON'T FOCUS ON THE PAST

> *Now the just shall live by faith; but if anyone draws back,*
> *my soul has no pleasure in him* (Hebrews 10:38 NKJV).

The realms and levels of life that God wants for us are in our future. We should not waste our time looking back so we don't become a monument that stands still and makes no progress. That's what happened to Lot's wife; she turned into a pillar of salt after she gazed longingly back at the place they had left.

Looking backward will hinder our forward progress. This is true in many areas of life, and it's true when we walk by faith. Looking back is not an option when we want to walk by faith. Looking forward gives us the anticipation and momentum we need to enter into the realms of life God has for us.

Paul wrote in Philippians 3:13 (NKJV), *"Brethren, I do not count myself to have apprehended; but one thing I do, forgetting those things which are behind and reaching forward to those things which are ahead."* The Greek meaning of the word for "forgetting" depicts the act of deliberately neglecting or losing something from our mind. This shows we must choose to deliberately neglect the things of the past and intentionally focus on our future. Someone said, "What you feed grows, and what you starve dies." To move to a new realm requires starving the old things of the past to death by neglecting to think about them and instead feeding on new thoughts about the future God has for us.

JESUS HAS CONQUERED EVERY REALM

Therefore He says: "When He ascended on high, He led captivity captive, and gave gifts to men." (Now this, "He ascended"—what does it mean but that He also first descended into the lower parts of the earth? He who descended is also the One who ascended far above all the heavens, that He might fill all things) (Ephesians 4:8-10 NKJV).

Jesus descended into the lowest realms and ascended into the highest realms that exist and established His lordship. Everywhere Jesus went, He conquered the opposition by winning them to His side or by defeating them. When Adam yielded to satan's temptation in the Garden, he gave up his right to be in charge of this earth and take care of it for God. Now satan had a right to establish his domain. But Jesus came into the earth and in His death, burial, and resurrection He took back all the devil had taken. He made a way for us to enter into every realm, dimension, and level of life to which He has called us.

We can go to any level of life that God directs us to go to. We have a legal right to be there because Jesus has gone before us to make a way for us. He has made room for us there. He will be there with you when you get there. He has prepared things for us at the level He wants us to be.

IT TAKES THE RIGHT MINDSET

God has also given us everything that is necessary to enter into the realms of life that He has promised us in His Word. He has given us the Word of God, the name of Jesus, the blood of Jesus, the anointing and power of the Holy Spirit, the whole armor of God, and faith in His Word. We must use these spiritual things if we're going to enter into new levels of life.

It is possible for us to live on a higher level than we do right now. However, it takes the right mindset, or right thinking, to use these spiritual things that God has given to us so we can enter into what He has promised. As we begin to think the thoughts of God's

Word, we will begin to see a whole new world opening up to us. Our horizons will be enlarged, and we'll see new possibilities and opportunities for us.

CHAPTER 14

DEVELOPING AN INCREASE MINDSET

"God's promises of increase have no age limits, so it's never too late to dream another dream and set another goal."

Years ago, I started a traveling ministry, but I couldn't seem to get many invitations to minister. The small amount of income we received that year was depressing. I was at a crossroads of whether to quit and do something else or get some help. I said to the Lord, "I'm doing what You told me to do. But I don't have many speaking engagements scheduled and our income isn't very much. The house we live in is so ugly we don't invite anyone to come over. My family isn't adequately dressed. Show me what to do." After praying I remained quiet and finally felt impressed to listen to some messages in which the speaker talked about developing an increase mentality. After several months of repeatedly listening to those messages and retraining my mind to think thoughts of increase, I began to receive more and better speaking engagements and my income started to go up as well.

Too often we've made our thought life our prison, barring us from living beyond the limits of our current circumstances. However, God will often call us beyond our current level of thinking into what He knows is possible for us. So we must be willing to change our mind to walk in God's plans.

OUR MIND MAY BE THE PROBLEM

Many people feel locked into the situation they're currently in and resign themselves to accept this as their lot in life. They look at others who have a better life than they do and wish they knew how to get more. Some who are in these situations resent the abundance or wealth that others have. I've heard some say about those who have more than most people that they were "born with a silver spoon in their mouth," meaning they had inherited their family wealth or had a rich benefactor.

Others shrug their shoulders and adopt the idea that God meant for certain families to have much and other families to have little. Too often the biggest problem for those who look at life this way is not their circumstances, but how their mind works and the thoughts they habitually entertain.

GOD HAS GIVEN US MANY PROMISES

There are many promises of God indicating that God is willing to give us more than we currently have. Jesus Himself said, *"I have come that they may have life, and that they may have it more abundantly"* (John 10:10 NKJV). For some, having more means having better health. Others need more freedom or more provision. Some are looking for better opportunities. We can have hope for tomorrow because God has promised us more.

God's promises include many things, both spiritual and natural. God will give us more grace and gives more wisdom to those who ask (James 4:6; 1:5). He desires that we abound more in love, knowledge, and discernment (Philippians 1:9). Jesus made it possible for us to be more than conquerors (Romans 8:37). God values us more than the birds and takes care of us more than any earthly father would (Luke 12:24; Matthew 7:11). He promised to give both us and our children more and more increase (Psalm 115:14). We're to desire God's Word more than anything else (Psalm 19:10), and He gives more to those who hear His Word (Mark 4:24).

THE LEVEL OF MORE THAN ENOUGH

Many people live on the level of barely enough, and for them every week has the potential to be a financial crisis. They go from paycheck to paycheck, living on the level of just enough with nothing for anything extra. Yet there are some people who always have more than enough to live on and fulfill their purpose in life. The fact that a person is born with a certain status in life doesn't mean that level is their inevitable fate in life or that they can't have increase no matter how hard they try.

Many of God's promises are conditional, meaning certain requirements have to be met in order to actually experience them. God's promises do not automatically show up in our lives. Unless we do something about our dreams and desires, they probably won't happen. Where we live is a choice we make daily—in the land of not enough, the land of just enough, or in the land of more than enough. Tomorrow will reflect what we have chosen to think and dream about today.

Jesus died on the Cross so that all the promises of God's Word are available to us (see 2 Corinthians 1:20). The Bible has a promise for every kind of need we may have. God wants us to live at the level of what He has promised in His Word.

To hear some people talk, you would think God couldn't afford to give us what we need or ask for. They act as if their request would thrust God into bankruptcy. But Colossians 1:16 tells us that God is the One who made everything. God has it all. The truth is, we must enlarge our thoughts to encompass who God really is, what He has, and what He wants to do for His children.

WEALTH AND INCREASE ARE AVAILABLE

There is plenty of wealth and resources in the earth for everyone. It is hard for the human mind to grasp the reality of all the minerals, precious metals, natural resources, plant and animal life, and fresh water in the earth. We can hardly imagine all that the earth is able to produce for the benefit of humankind.

A number of globalists and world leaders believe the human population level has or is in danger of passing the earth's sustainable rate of providing for the needs of people and are concerned that earth's resources will run out. While we should make efforts to conserve our earthly resources, neither should we live in fear that there isn't or will not be enough for everyone.

There are great amounts of wealth and resources in the earth that man has not yet discovered. Over seventy percent of the earth's surface is underwater, and there are vast riches in these underwater areas that have yet to be discovered and put into use for the benefit of humankind. Great efforts are being made by marine biologists and others to explore the bottom of the ocean, which has been referred to as "Earth's Final Frontier." They are developing equipment that can withstand the water pressure at the deepest depths of the ocean so they can continue to learn about the valuable things there.

Trillions of dollars are in the hands of American people, which reveals that great wealth does exist. However most of those trillions of dollars are in the hands of a small percentage of Americans. So the non-existence of wealth is not the problem. The issue is that many don't know how to get their share of the resources and wealth that is available. Wealth and increase does not come automatically or just because people need something. It comes to those who know how to appropriate it into our lives.

ABUNDANCE TO ACCOMPLISH OUR MISSION

God did not miscalculate when He created the earth and all of its resources and riches. After the flood, God promised Noah, *"While the earth remains, seedtime and harvest, cold and heat, winter and summer, and day and night shall not cease. ...Every moving thing that lives shall be food for you. I have given you all things, even as the green herbs"* (Genesis 8:22; 9:3 NKJV).

The psalmist showed the importance of being one of God's people when he said, *"For the Lord has chosen Zion; He has desired it for His dwelling place: 'This is My resting place forever; here I will dwell, for I have desired it. I will abundantly bless her provision; I will satisfy her poor with bread'"* (Psalm 132:13-15 NKJV). Zion is a type of the Church, referring to those who are born again and are the people of God, no matter what their denomination may be. God has assured us in His Word that He desires to provide abundantly for us (see Matthew 6:33; 7:11; John 10:10).

We must become aware of the wealth and increase that is available to us before we can have it. As Christians, we are members of the most affluent family in the universe—the family of God. We are the reason God put all this wealth in the earth. God had the well-being of humanity in mind as He created the earth and all that He put in it. He has made an invisible reservoir of abundance and wealth that we can tap into when we activate the spiritual laws in the Word. As Christians who want to obey God, we need to believe God wants us to have wealth and increase so we can fulfill the Great Commission God has given to us to reach the world for Christ.

PREPARE FOR SUPERNATURAL INCREASE

Reading the progress of Israel throughout its history shows us many parallels with the development and advancement of the Church today. Isaiah, the great Messianic prophet, spoke of the future of Israel:

> *Enlarge the place of your tent, and let them stretch out the curtains of your dwellings; do not spare; lengthen your cords, and strengthen your stakes. For you shall expand to the right and to the left, and your descendants will inherit the nations, and make the desolate cities inhabited* (Isaiah 54:2-3 NKJV).

This is a direct reference to the Jews after they return from captivity and a prophecy of increase for their nation after they had resettled in their own land. Here's what happened after Isaiah spoke this prophecy. The number of people who came out of Babylon was a little over 42,000 (see Ezra 2:64). Some five hundred years later, just before the destruction of Jerusalem by the Romans, they had greatly increased. Going by the calculation of the Passover lambs used, a conservative estimate of the number of Jewish people at that time was around 3 million.

Within the next five centuries after Isaiah 54:2-3 was spoken, the Jewish people experienced a time of great increase; it was an explosion of growth. So the early part of this prophecy has already come to pass, which gives hope for a latter fulfillment in the end times when God again draws Israel back to Himself and their eyes are reopened to see Jesus Christ as their Messiah and become born again.

THESE VERSES SPEAK PROPHETICALLY

Prophetically, these verses also speak of the Church. In the book of Acts we read how the Church began on the Day of Pentecost, beginning with only one hundred twenty followers in the Upper Room and in that one day exploding to over three thousand people from many different nations (see Acts 2:41). Later it grew to over five thousand (see Acts 4:4), and from there the Church expanded into Judea, Samaria, and to the uttermost parts of the earth. Yet that is still not the whole picture, for these verses speak not only of the early Church in its beginning stages, but to the Church of every generation until the return of Jesus Christ.

THESE VERSES ARE FOR US TODAY

These verses reveal that God has plans of increase for us, just as He did for Israel and the early Church. Therefore, we must prepare our attitudes and actions so we are ready for the increase that God is speaking about. Isaiah 54:2 contains instructions for God's people to follow, and Isaiah 54:3 contains God's promise of increase for them. At a time of great difficulty and while Israel was in an impossible situation that no human power could fix, Isaiah delivered God's promise of a time of great increase for Israel. Although God spoke specifically to Israel in these verses, yet the promise is just as applicable to God's people today.

Israel had to do some things to get ready for the time of increase that God spoke of in this verse. We should pay close attention to what God told Israel, as these are lessons we can learn on how to prepare for the increase God wants us to have. Increase can be a blessing and not a curse if we prepare for it. Specifically, there are five phrases used in these verses that reveal how to get ready for increase. These instructions are types of the New Testament actions that God's people should take today.

Enlarge!

One meaning of the word *enlarge* is to broaden or to make room for something. For Israel, this phrase instructs them to enlarge their hearts and minds to believe that a time is coming when their numbers would again increase and they would need larger dwelling places.

Today, for us this phrase indicates to broaden or make room in our mind and heart to embrace the many promises God has given to us in His Word. We are to enlarge our mind with the thoughts of God and believe in our hearts what God wants to do in our life and ministry. This paints a picture within us of receiving increase in our life, both spiritually and naturally.

Stretch Out!

The words *stretch out* indicate the idea of spreading out, extending, or reaching out. Here, God instructs Israel to embrace the idea that their current living space is not enough and they must make room for more. They must extend the walls of their dwellings, both spiritually and naturally, to encompass the increase God will bring to them.

In the same way, we must stretch out or extend our thinking and believing to include God's promises of increase. This means we must think beyond our former thought levels. It means that we must move outside our comfort zone. Moving out from where we would normally go and exploring new places can help enlarge our thinking. Sometimes it helps us to get around people who have dared to do greater things than we have done. Looking for environments that will lift us to a higher level of thinking, vision, and performance will help us be prepared for increase.

Do Not Spare!

This phrase carries the meaning of sparing no expenses, to do something at all costs, or do something without any reservations on their part. This attitude is necessary in preparing for increase. The Israelites were not to draw back in unbelief at the word the prophet brought to them. They should not spare any effort, energy, or resources in embracing the increase God promised to bring to them. Their children would become numerous once again and they would need to expand their natural borders to accommodate the growth. This required them to expand their thinking of what was possible for them.

Like the Israelites, we too must change our thinking to include the promises of God for our lives. We should not draw back in unbelief that God cannot bring increase to our lives. We must use our thoughts and imaginations to meditate upon the possibilities of God's Word coming to pass in our lives. This may mean being willing to use our money and resources to prepare for the increase God has for us.

Lengthen!

The word *lengthen* speaks of extending, drawing out, or prolonging something. The Israelites had to extend their cords to hold up bigger tents to accommodate their numerical growth. What worked with a small tent would not work with a larger tent. They also had to lengthen their thoughts to embrace the geographical territory that God would give to them as a place to live.

Often we need to lengthen our thoughts to accept God's promises of increase into our lives. Our current thought patterns and imaginations need to be enlarged or lengthened to be in agreement with God's plans of increase. Too often our thoughts and imaginations limit us in what we think we can do or what would be possible for us.

For example, a dog tied to a post with a cord or chain is limited in his activities, resources, and provision. What the dog needs may be just beyond the length of the cord to which he is tied, but he can't reach it. Therefore, he is limited in what he can experience in life. Thoughts are the links in the chains that determine our level of existence and achievement in life. We are either limited by thoughts that discourage us from having what God promised or released by thoughts large enough to enable us to reach the goals and the potential to which God has called us.

We must be careful we don't make our thoughts a prison that we live in. So we need to open our mind to what God said in His Word that He is able to do for His children. When we grasp in our thoughts the great quantity of God's resources and begin to meditate upon the wealth in this earth that is available for our well-being, then the castles of old thinking will be torn down and we'll be able see the possibility of living in increase.

Strengthen!

The final phrase of instruction to the Israelites reveals the crux of the matter—the part that causes everything else to be successful. The word *strengthen* gives the idea of fortifying, being strong, being courageous, or being obstinate. For a tent to remain standing in all kinds of weather, especially in times of adversity, it must depend upon the strength of the stakes to which the tent ropes are tied. In a prophetic sense, this word means to strengthen in order to prevail, to seize, or to conquer something. This speaks of the necessity of building a certain mindset or having a set of attitudes so Israel could believe and begin to act on God's prophetic word of increase to them.

So the critical issue is to fortify our mind with the Word of God and continue to meditate until we see the increase God has promised. To strengthen our stakes gives the idea of consistently building up our ability to form Bible-based attitudes until our mind becomes a castle that won't be moved away from the Word of God. To receive what God has promised to us in both good and bad times depends upon us being courageous, conquering, established, and prevailing in our thought life.

THE DEVIL TRIES TO CAPTURE OUR MIND

Satan will bring adversity against us, especially after we step out to receive God's promise of increase in some area of our life. In the Parable of the Sower, Jesus said satan comes to steal the Word from those who hear it (see Mark 4:15). He wants to steal the Word out of our life so we have nothing left to stand on. He wants us to move away from what God is saying to us. If the devil can take over our thought life, he has obtained a great victory.

So we must continually feed upon God's Word until our mind and heart are firmly established with God's thoughts. We must never let up on our spiritual progress, being diligent to *"give no place to the devil"* in our thought life (Ephesians 4:27 NKJV). Then satan can't find a foothold to enter into our thought life, and we'll be able to hold on to God's promises of increase that belong to us.

God instructed Israel ahead of time to prepare for increase numerically and geographically. This prophetic word spoke of a time to come. The greatest preparation Israel could undertake was to get their minds and hearts to consistently and unwaveringly think and believe they could have God's promise of numerical and geographical growth.

After we hear God's promise of increase, we must continually feed that promise into our hearts and minds by meditating on it. This positions us to capitalize on the increase God wants to bring to us in other areas of our lives. Then we will begin to break forth on every hand. The things that were desolate, barren, and didn't produce anything can flourish once again and bring forth abundance. Some will ask what happened to us, and we'll be able to say, "The Lord did this for me when I obeyed His Word, and He'll do it for you too."

Growing into the Things of God

Unless God chooses to do something miraculous, change in our soul happens through a process over a period of time. As we apply the principles of renewing our mind, conforming our will, and controlling our emotions, we will grow ourselves into the things of God.

Sometimes I tell my wife, "Let's grow ourselves into what God is saying." This means that we're going to change the condition of our souls, which will then enable us to experience what God has told us. How do we go about implementing the process of growing ourselves into what God has for us? Here is a quick synopsis of how we can grow ourselves into living in God's promises:

First, we search the Word for Scriptures that apply to the areas we need to grow in. We continually read and meditate upon these Scriptures until they become a part of us. We know they are a part of us when they show up in our talk and in our walk. We feed on these Scriptures until we're overflowing with expectations and declarations of a successful outcome in our situation. Luke 6:45 (NKJV) tells us that *"out of the abundance of the heart his mouth speaks."*

Second, we listen to people who have teaching products to gain knowledge in the areas we need to grow. We go to seminars and conferences when we can. We make sure that our spiritual and mental diet reflects the level of life we want to have and what we want to accomplish. Then, mentally and emotionally, we can embrace God's plan before we actually experience it.

If it's possible, we find those who have already gone through what we're going through to see what they did to have a successful outcome. These individuals can share truths and principles from their experiences that will save us many steps and hours of labor. The reason the different incidents in the lives of the Israelites and other people in the Bible were recorded is so we can learn from them (see 1 Corinthians 10:11).

Third, during this time of growing we also listen to the Holy Spirit to see what He has to say about our situation. He sees and knows all things. He is able to guide us into the perfect will of God,

207

which is in agreement with God's written Word. We are alert to any Scriptures the Holy Spirit may quicken to our spirit or bring to our attention to show us what He wants to do and what He wants us to do.

Fourth, we go to meetings where God's presence and glory is being manifested. Being in the presence of God's glory helps us go beyond the level of thinking we had before and frees us to think higher thoughts. There we're able to receive God's thoughts, change our thinking, and embrace the changes God wants us to make with the least amount of resistance in our mind.

A Prosperous Soul Is the Key

When we grow ourselves into the things of God by changing the conditions of our soul, we develop the right mindset to operate in the different things the Word of God tells us to do. Then we can pray according to God's will, exercise faith in His Word, and operate in the laws of sowing and reaping. Then we can move with God's Spirit and flow with Him as He directs us and become a channel through which God can bring help and blessings to others.

Many need God to move miraculously for them. If God doesn't do miracles for them, they have no answers or solutions. However, unless a person prepares themselves to receive God's miracles by renewing their mind to His thoughts and ways, they may not be in a position to recognize, receive, or maintain what God is doing for them.

"Beloved, I pray that you may prosper in all things and be in health, just as your soul prospers" (3 John 1:2 NKJV). Increase in any area of our lives begins when we change the condition of our soul.

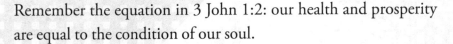

Remember the equation in 3 John 1:2: our health and prosperity are equal to the condition of our soul.

Sometimes we must wait upon God to get direction or experience God's anointing. There are times when we need God to perform a miracle for us because nothing else will supply what we need. But often we can simply grow ourselves into the things of God by changing the condition of our soul. As we do, God will bless us with all He has promised us in His Word.

MOVE UP TO THE NEXT LEVEL

Many Christians don't receive the inheritance that God's Word tells them they can have because they never grow up. In the natural, babies, children, and even teenagers are often not prepared to deal wisely and appropriately with large amounts of wealth or increase. They either spend it all in a short period of time or ruin their lives by purchasing things that are detrimental to them. Unless we grow up and change the condition of our soul, we are not able to receive the inheritance God meant for us to have.

I heard the story of a very wealthy couple who found out they could not have any children. However, they kept believing God's Word and meditating on God's promises in that area. Finally after a number of years, they did have a child. One day after the child was several years old, the father lifted the child up and said, "I can't wait for you to grow up so I can show you my world!"

God wants His children to grow up so He can show them His world. He desires to give what He has to His children. He wants to see His children blessed. Believe and declare that today is not a life sentence with God; He desires for us to move on up to new levels in life!

REVOLUTIONARY MINDSET PRINCIPLES

1. When we dream of things greater than our circumstances, it doesn't have to be in vain. That's how all great things begin; now all that's left is to build it.

2. Obstacles can be conquered, for they are as big as they will ever get. But we can overcome them because we can keep on growing.

3. The purpose of life is not to see how long we can live but the difference we can make.

4. God created the human soul to be a great repository out of which we can mine great riches.

5. A human is distinct from all other creatures by having a soul with rational thoughts and expressions, which must be brought under the divine instruction of God to move in the right direction.

6. Our greatest support and our worst hindrances are the thoughts we choose to entertain about ourselves.

7. Our world has become the way it is by the habitual thoughts we have entertained, and it cannot be changed until we change what we think.

8. Truly great accomplishments don't happen spontaneously—they often happen through a series of small things that someone exercises their will to do.

9. The most important thing an individual can do is obey God's will and pray, "God, Your will be done."

10. Our human emotions want to be our masters, and often we unconsciously submit to them.

11. Don't allow yourself to be sabotaged by your emotions; instead, use them for your benefit.

12. Jesus knows what we have been through, and He can heal every hurt, remove every sorrow, and help us in every situation.

13. Unless we get God's Word in us, our thoughts will continue to reflect the world around us.

14. Building thoughts of faith in our mind and heart helps us to trust in God's big plans even though we may not totally understand them.

15. Our thoughts in the past have brought us into the present world; our thoughts today will also help us step into our future.

16. God's promises of increase have no age limits, so it's never too late to dream another dream and set another goal.

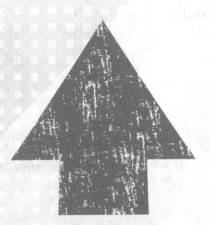

PRAYER TO RECEIVE SALVATION

The greatest gift you could ever receive from God is the salvation of your soul. If you desire to receive forgiveness of your sins and make Jesus Christ the Lord of your life, pray the following prayer and mean it with all your heart:

Heavenly Father, Your Word says, "whoever calls on the name of the Lord shall be saved" (Romans 10:13 NKJV). Your Word also says that, "if you confess with your mouth the Lord Jesus and believe in your heart that God has raised Him from the dead, you will be saved" (Romans 10:9 NKJV). I call upon You today, and I ask You to become my Lord and Savior. Please forgive me of all my sins. Thank You for the blood of Jesus Christ washing me clean and pure from all my sins. I now confess Jesus is my Lord and Savior. I believe I am now born again. I am now a child of God. Thank You, heavenly Father, for receiving me as a member in Your family, in Jesus' name. Amen.

If you have prayed that prayer to receive salvation, I encourage you to find a Bible-believing church to attend so you can begin to grow up into all God has for you.

If you desire to contact us to let us know you prayed this prayer, you may contact us by email at marvin@marvinyoder.org.